# CHOICES

# CHOICES

## Making Right Decisions in a Complex World

### LEWIS B. SMEDES

*1817*

Harper & Row, Publishers, San Francisco

Cambridge, Hagerstown, New York, Philadelphia, Washington
London, Mexico City, São Paulo, Singapore, Sydney

FIRST EDITION.

_____

**Library of Congress Cataloging-in-Publication Data**

Smedes, Lewis B.
  Choices: making right decisions in a complex world.

  1. Conduct of life.  I. Title.
BJ1581.2.S55   1986                      170'.44                    86-45025
ISBN 0-06-067415-6

_____

86  87  88  89  90  RRD  10  9  8  7  6  5  4  3  2  1

*To My Students*
*at Fuller Seminary*

# CONTENTS

To the wise men and women of times past and present from whom I have harvested almost every thought in this volume,

To my friends Richard Mouw, Linda Smith, and Doris Smedes, who have read and criticized my manuscript,

To my students who have let me share these thoughts with them from time to time,

To my editors, Linda Mead of L. T. Mead & Associates and Roy M. Carlisle of Harper & Row San Francisco,

To readers of other books of mine who have lured me into believing that writing still another might be useful,

To my Lord,

I give my sincere thanks.

Sierra Madre, 1986

# Foreword

We all make choices that touch other people's lives, as well as our own, in ways that leave us wondering whether we are really doing the right thing.

A strange inner force now and then trips us into asking ourselves, "But is it right?" This force, this hormone of our conscience, does not let us stifle it for long; it may sleep for a while, but eventually, when doubt lingers on after the act is done, it wakes up and sneaks into our minds as a creeping disquiet, a vexing misgiving that we might have done the wrong thing.

Sooner or later, most of us have a personal rendezvous with a trembling hunch that we have made a wrong choice.

But how do we know what is right and what is wrong?

Is morality all hit and miss? A matter of how you were brought up? How folks felt about things in your part of the world? Does the question of right and wrong always come down in the end to a matter of taste? When it comes to taste, the sage said, there can be no arguments; to each his own. Is morality like that; whatever each of us happens to feel good about or what others of us have no stomach for?

Or is there some real sense to morality?

Can we talk together about morality as reasonable persons, listen to each other, compare our thoughts, and come to some rational conclusions about the choices we make? I think we can. Morality in my view is not something that we can only shout at each other about. We can consider each other's arguments, weigh them, agree and disagree with them, present alternative points of view, and help each other see things more clearly than we did before. We can reason together about moral choices as rationally as we can with any other choices we make.

Some of us feel comfortable only if all the questions we have about right and wrong are settled by an authority. So we trust morality to the experts, to prophets and priests or gurus and savants, who are supposed to really know what is right and what is wrong. We look for somebody to tell us for sure. What we want—especially in our complicated culture where everything seems up for grabs, where many of our traditional convictions are challenged—is assurance. We don't want discussions, we want declarations.

People who take their morality only from authority figures tend to feel shortchanged if the answer they get is fudged. When they are looking for a clear and undeniable word on a sticky matter and someone bedevils the issue with a bothersome "But on the other hand, have you considered . . .?" they become unsettled and begin to look for another authority, one who really knows. They want it straight and they want it final, so they can know where they stand. What else are authorities for?

But now and then we run into crises that our authorities have no definite answer for. Or if they do have one, their clear answer runs smack against the clear answer of other authorities. Or against life as we live it.

I serve on the ethics committee of a great hospital in southern California where choices made almost every day determine the life and death of very sick people. These are crises that keep serious doctors awake at night wondering whether they are making the right choices. But very often no one has a clear and simple answer.

Is it right to stop expensive treatment of an elderly patient when the machine seems to be keeping a body alive after the person who once lived in it has gone? Is it right not to operate on a newborn baby when all indications are that the baby will exist as a virtual vegetable even if the operation is successful? When we face questions like these in the form of real people about whose lives we are deciding, we need to reason together with utmost respect for each other's ways of looking at each case.

There is no place like a hospital to discover that there is more than one way to look at moral choices.

Now and then we all get into situations that seem to tell us that we are "damned if we do and damned if we don't." Other occasions seem to tell us that there simply is no right or wrong thing to do about them, but only a somewhat better thing, or a less bad thing. These are times when we feel as if we are thrown on our own, and we may end up wondering whether *anyone* can know for sure that he or she has made a right choice.

We need to think about *how* we can know, maybe not for sure, but at least with good reasons to support our decisions.

I invite you to carry on a discussion with me, and with your-self, about making right choices. About how to evaluate our choices, how to tell right ones from wrong ones, better ones from worse ones. About how to challenge conventional wisdom and popular notions. About how to make up your own mind on what is right.

If you want to be preached to about what is wrong with this, that, and the other thing, you have the wrong book in your hands. This one doesn't do that. It is about how to judge for yourself, in a rational and responsible way, about the moral choices you make.

Of course, wiser people than either of us have been thinking about morality for a long time. There is a long history of thought behind this little book; mostly I am just a conduit for great ideas of greater minds than mine. But I did not write the book to teach you what the teachers tell us. Instead, I want to help you to work through the process for yourself.

Everyone who thinks about moral choices looks at life with his or her own slant. We all have a faith, a way of seeing things, a point of view. My own faith is Christian; you will notice that sooner or later.

I am personally thankful, however, that we live together in a large moral house even if we do not drink at the same fountain of faith. The world we experience together is one world, God's world, and our world, and the problems we share are common human problems. So we can talk together, try to understand each other, and help each other.

In short, this book is about how anyone at all can know whether he or she is making right choices in a confusing world where there always seems to be at least one other way of looking at any problem.

So join me and let's reason together, one step at a time, about the choices we make, especially the choices that sometimes leave us wondering, "Did I do the right thing?"

CHAPTER 1

# What's Good about Being Right?

It feels good. But is it right?
It looks good. But is it right?
It pays well. But is it right?

One question weaves its pesky way through everything we do. It tags behind us. It nags inside us. It sneaks into our consciousness, usually uninvited and often unwanted, and it will not quit its dogged pursuit of our best and truest selves. The question is: Are we doing the *right* thing?

We ask it when we want to be sure about a decision we must make tomorrow. We ask it when we feel a remnant of trembling doubt about a choice we made yesterday.

It bothers us, it annoys us; we often wish we could shake it off and do whatever we want whenever the mood is on us— double our pleasure or double our money—and away with the nagging question of right or wrong. But we cannot walk away from it. Not the way we can walk away from the newspaper and the TV set. For it echoes from the abyss of our being. It is the voice of our most real self.

Of course, we are talking about a special kind of right and wrong; and we may as well label it with the proper word, that indelicate word, that nuisance word, that unsociable word, *moral*.

We all twit each other about the right and wrong of almost everything people do, but mostly we are talking about something that has nothing at all to do with morality.

Take a few examples. You could be wearing clashing colors; your choice of colors is *aesthetically* wrong. But only an idiot would suggest that you are morally wrong because your colors are wrong. You may invest in a losing mutual fund; your choice is *economically* wrong. But you are not morally wrong for making a bad investment. You could drive sixty miles an hour in a forty-mile zone when taking your spouse to the hospital; you would be *legally* wrong. But nobody in his or her right mind will tell you that you are being morally wrong for breaking a traffic law when you think your spouse's life could be in the balance. So, you can do any number of things that are wrong in other ways and still be home free in the moral world.

The same sorts of differences filter through the word "right." We can wear the right clothes to a party, buy the right stock, go to the right therapist, attend the right church, have a smashing sex life, and still, on the moral stage, hobble like a ballet dancer on crutches.

If you filmed a single scene from ordinary life, and showed it to a bunch of ordinary people, you might get a flock of different slants on the right or wrong of what was going on, each of them coming from a legitimate vantage point, yet all of them missing the moral factor.

Take this little story, for instance.

Two people are waiting for a bus. The first person in line is a slight little lady, maybe ninety pounds or so, about sixty-five years old, carrying her dignity along with a bag full of groceries. The second person is a young man, about eighteen, a big chunk of a fellow, maybe two hundred pounds. The little lady climbs aboard the bus first. She struggles down the aisle and gets about halfway to the back of the bus before she notices that there is only one empty seat in the bus, and it is the center seat in the rear row. The strapping young man spots the empty seat too, and he bolts for it. He muscles past the elderly lady, elbows her to one side, sends her sprawling over a couple of persons' laps, lettuce and potatoes rolling down the aisle. She is shocked and breathless, but not seriously injured. The young man sits down in the empty seat and looks straight ahead.

Their fellow passengers are watching. They all find fault with what the young man did, and a few of them grumble their complaints.

A ballet teacher grumps, "How clumsy he was." She sees something aesthetically wrong.

An elegant lady huffs, "What bad taste to do a thing like that in public." She sees it as a breach of etiquette, a misdemeanor roughly equivalent to burping in church.

A lawyer with pince-nez glasses gripes, "I'm sure there's a rule against doing that." He sees something legally wrong with what the young man did.

A wizened orthopedist in patched tweed gives an instant diagnosis, "I think she may have fractured a rib." He sees something medically wrong.

A natty psychologist looks up from her copy of *The New Yorker* and muses, "The lad acts like a sociopath; he must be sick." She sees something psychologically wrong.

Suppose you were sitting in the bus, and suppose you knew what these people were thinking. You would probably fume, "These people are missing the most important point. It is not that the young man was clumsy, or in poor taste, or illegal, or neurotic, or even whether the woman cracked a rib. The important thing is that what he did was *morally* wrong."

He did something that nobody ought to do to another person, especially if she had done no wrong to him, even more so if she was weaker than he was and had no defense. What he did was unfair, it was unkind, cruel, and this is why it was morally wrong.

So when we say it was morally wrong we mean that he *ought* not to have done it. In some special sense, some terribly serious sense, he ought not to have done what he did. If he had been as graceful as a prancing fawn, and legal as a government bond, he still ought not to have done it. What he did was wrong in that strange and troublesome sense we call morally wrong.

More, when we judge that what the young man on the bus did was wrong, we probably mean that *no one* ought to do that sort of thing. We do not mean that it was wrong only for this crude clod to do what he did. It would be wrong for anyone, anywhere, anytime, period.

We have gotten close to what we mean when we say that something is morally wrong or morally right.

Morality is all about how we treat people, including ourselves. Treating people unfairly and unlovingly—this is what moral wrong is. Treating people fairly and lovingly—this is what moral right is.

Morality is about doing things to people that result in their rights being respected and their needs being tended to. It is not about living up to customs and traditions. It is not about fitting into society's traditional values. Morality is only about living in a way that respects people's rights and cares for people's needs.

This tells us what's good about being right. Being morally right is good for people. Or, to put it in reverse, being good for people is what being morally right is all about. And hurting people needlessly is what being morally wrong is all about.

Mind you, though, being morally wrong is not the same as displeasing people or making them angry. And doing the right thing—in the moral sense—is not the same as doing things that please people.

I know people who feel guilty whenever they displease someone, especially someone important to them. They may spend their entire lives trying to please their mothers, for example, and even when mother is dead and gone, they still feel guilty whenever they do something that would have made her feel badly. They confuse morality with pleasing people, and the confusion leaves them feeling guilty when they may be innocent as a baby chick.

We need to say the same thing about doing the right thing; being in the right morally is not the same as making people feel comfortable. A con artist can charm us into sweet comfort for a while, but when we discover we've been cheated, we know for sure that being a charmer is not the same as being moral.

In fact, doing the right thing can make a lot of people very uncomfortable. Martin Luther King, Jr., set many people's teeth on edge; the original Martin Luther rocked powerful people down to their souls' heels. And we know what happened to Jesus. Being good to people does not always make them feel good.

Why should we mince the matter? The plain-spoken fact is this: if you do right, in the moral sense, you will not please all of the people all of the time.

That settled, and before we go on, we need to settle a fundamental question, a life and death question as far as right and wrong are concerned. Go back to the young hulk on the bus for a moment, and recall what he did to the woman. Was it really wrong? I mean, was what he *did* wrong? Was the wrongness of it a quality of what he did—the way a ballet dancer's pirouette has the quality of grace and a thoroughbred's run for the roses has the quality of speed? Or was its wrongness only inside our private feeling about what we saw?

Is this all that morality is about—strong feelings about things? Not liking things? Hating things? When you say, "It was wrong for Mr. Oswald to shoot President Kennedy," do you mean nothing more than when you utter a deep-felt "Ugh" on hearing a revolting joke?

If you say that a father was wrong for abusing his daughter, do you mean only to let us know that you do not like what he did? Are you reporting on your upset stomach or are you trying to tell us that, in your opinion, what he *did* was wrong?

We disagree about right and wrong, of course, and why not, since we have at one time or other disagreed about almost everything else. Terrorists may believe they are doing right when they highjack an airplane and kill passengers in cold blood. You may believe they are doing a terrible wrong against humanity. So you and the terrorists disagree. Does the fact that you and the terrorists do not see eye to eye mean that neither of you can be correct?

Come now, let us reason together: Do we live in a world where nobody is ever really right or really wrong?

Is human life a moral hodgepodge, a bedlam of conflicting feelings, where nobody's opinion on right and wrong is ever any closer to the truth than anyone else's opinion? I don't think so. In fact, the worst thing we can do for the human family, in my opinion, is to leave right and wrong up to everybody's sovereign gut feelings.

Don't we sense the moral factor in life, when it comes down to it, the way we sense that a solid rock we stubbed our toe on is real and not an illusion? For most of us, it is an intuition we could not deny if we wanted to. We cannot wash it out of our souls anymore than the ocean can wash away its own abysmal bottom; it is as natural to us as it is natural to hear the sound of music or to capture the image of sunset at sea. We see morality in life simply because our humanity is in touch with a deep design for how human beings are meant to treat each other.

Maybe it will help if we go over all this again, once more, lightly. Remember that if you agree with the following, you will have made one of the most important decisions about human existence that you will ever make.

Morality is about treating people fairly and lovingly. When we say we *ought* to do right, we really mean that we ought to treat people right.

Rightness and wrongness are real qualities of human actions, and not merely private prejudices we happen to have about them.

We intuit the moral dimension in human life because we still have the sense for genuine humanity that God created us with.

Our intuition does not send us an infallible message of what is right and what is wrong in specific cases. For that, we need some clear thinking about moral standards and how to apply them to real life.

Well now, having claimed that the moral factor is a real and a critical dimension in our common lives, a factor fatal to everything good if we neglect it, we need to look at the other side of the picture: morality isn't everything.

For goodness sake, we shouldn't saturate life with morality. You can ruin the fun of living if you overload it with morality.

Some things are just for the fun—or the pain—of them. They do not cut any moral ice; they are neutral, neither here nor there in the moral catalogue. They exist only for us to experience them. And celebrate them. Sometimes suffer them. We mustn't spoil our pleasure—or add to our pain—by seeing moral issues in everything people do.

There is a time to sing and dance, to love and wonder, to play and work, touch our bodies and feel the wind only for the sheer joy of it. A time definitely not to give a passing thought to the right and wrong of things.

If we are not morally serious at all, we eventually turn the human family into a rat pack. But if we are morally serious about everything, we transpose the song of life too soon into a sorrow-shot dirge.

Another thing worth remembering about the moral side of life is this: some things do not matter as much as other things. Some people respond to what they do, or to what other people do as if when something they do is wrong, it is wrong, period, and is as bad as bad can be. No shadings, no nuances, no degrees. If it is at all wrong, paint it pitch-black.

People like this can do a lot of harm, especially if they have a hand in bringing up children. They rear children who grow up without a feel for the important difference between a moral peccadillo and a moral felony, and who feel as guilty about a minor slip into a small fault as they do over a major assault on human fairness and decency. So, obvious as it may seem to our minds, the point needs to sink into our feelings: some wrong things are worse than other wrong things. Just as some good things are better than other good things.

Consider some comparisons, and test them on your own scale. Is it worse to abuse a child than to cheat on income taxes? Is it worse to malign a neighbor than to lie a little by telling somebody that he looks great when you think that he looks a mess? Is it worse to let starving people die than to chop down a redwood tree in a national park? Is it worse to practice racism than to have sex with the wrong person?

Well, that's enough, I think, to establish the obvious: morality is not monotony. In terms of how serious they are, two moral matters can be as far apart as a polliwog is from a whale.

Before leaving this subject, we need to say something about what morality has to do with God. Or what God has to do with morality.

The first thing to say is that if there is a free and intelligent divine Being who created a world populated with free and intelligent human beings, you would expect such a God to have a rather clear idea of how he meant his free and intelligent creatures to live together and treat each other in his world.

But suppose this Creator is as loving as he is intelligent. Suppose, in fact, that down to the beating heart of his divine being, he *is* love. Wouldn't it follow that whatever his mind planned for us would include the good his love would want for us? So, when we choose to live by his intelligent design we are also choosing what is best for us all in the long run. And this is what morality is all about.

Morality is user-friendly, humane, a signal pointing us to what is best for our true selves. This is what's good about being right.

CHAPTER 2

# Sorting out the Categories

At my school, students can, if they choose, take a few courses on a pass/fail option. In these courses, they either pass or fail, and that's that, as far as the record shows.

But no one can gauge a student's real performance in a course by the sheer fact that he passed or failed it. He could pass with honors and he could pass by the skin of his academic teeth. He could fail wholesale or he could miss success by a hair breadth.

In the same way, morality is too complex to be jammed into categories labeled "right" and "wrong."

We know, for instance, that sometimes the difference between choices people make is only that one is better than the other, or not as bad as the other, not that one is simply right and the other is simply wrong. As a matter of fact, we have a fairly large repertoire of categories for expressing our moral opinions.

For instance:

"What my ex-husband did to me is *unforgivable!*"
"I cannot *excuse* you for telling your filthy stories at my party, even if you did have too much to drink."
"We will not *tolerate* the sale of pornography in our town."
"Everyone is *obligated* to keep his or her promise."
"God does not *permit* people to spoil the environment."
"Mother Teresa does *superb* work."

Comments like these reveal a few of the shadings in the moral landscape of our lives. They remind us of life's wonderful, and sometimes tragic, complexity.

I suggest that we look a little deeper now into some of the different categories we all use. I will introduce each of them with the sort of question anyone is likely to ask about it.


## IS IT FORGIVABLE?

Forgiving someone is a gracious way to cope with personal pain in a world where people hurt each other unfairly. When we forgive, we transcend the pain we feel by surrendering our right to get even with the person who hurt us.

But there is a judgmental side to forgiving: No one ever forgives a person without blaming him first.

If you betray me by telling someone the secret I trusted you with—telling it, in fact to someone who may use it against me— I will judge what you did as a wrong before I ever get around to forgiving you for it. The equation goes like this: If we do not judge something to be wrong, we do not need to forgive the person who did it.

Thus, we make two judgments whenever we forgive people: we believe that they did something unfair to us, and we hold them personally responsible.

When we decide that someone is forgivable, we conclude that what that person did was not too evil and did not slice too deeply into the flesh of humanity to fit within the forgiving zone.

Take rape, for instance. Nobody forgives a rapist easily, ever. We feel his immense wrong too ferociously. And our deep doubts about whether anyone should ever forgive him match our outrage at his evil.

But we are not quick to consign a lover's lapse or a friend's neglect into the everlasting fires of unforgivability. The wrongness of them does not cut so deep a gash into our moral flesh.

The other judgment we make is that people who hurt us are responsible for what they do. They did not have to do it. The pain they caused was not written in the stars or in their genetic codes. They are to blame. If we forgive people at all, we forgive them precisely because we hold them accountable.

Of course, you may believe that nothing is ever unforgivable because since God's mercy has no boundaries, neither should ours. But then you are not shaving a millimeter off the wrong people are sometimes responsible for. You are only stretching the mercy zone very wide.

## IS IT EXCUSABLE?

We excuse people when we decide that we should not blame them for what they did. We have already decided that what they did was wrong. But now we also decide that they were not responsible for what they did.

What do we do when we excuse someone?

We relax our judgment on that person. Or at least we temper it—to some extent. And so we decide not to blame or punish him or her. We still believe that wrong was done. We just do not hold this person accountable for doing it.

Excusing people is usually a matter of degree. We can excuse them completely, or halfway, or just a small way. That is, we may let them totally off the hook. Or we may say they bear only a share of guilt. Excusing is never an exact science.

We excuse people when we understand that they were not in control of their actions. They could not help doing what they did. Something in them or outside of them made them do it; they could not choose, and to that extent they were not free to act differently.

One night, not long ago, a good friend of mine drove up a hill behind his house and shot himself. He should not have done it. He brought unspeakable pain and loss to his wife. He catapulted his sons and daughters into soul-wrenching agony and doubt. Being a doctor, he robbed many sick people of his healing skills.

What my friend did was wrong.

But we who knew him well could imagine the deep depression that must have engulfed him in a black night of hopelessness. We could believe that, in his state, he could do nothing but surrender to despair. And he fell, he did not leap, into death's seduction.

We excused him. We toned down our judgments. Some of us did not judge him at all.

We are also—usually—willing to excuse people, at least partly, because of extenuating circumstances. Maybe a man poisoned his wife because she had Alzheimer's disease and he wanted to relieve her of the indignity of a slow slide into mind-less infancy. Maybe a father shot a man who had assaulted his family. Sometimes the circumstances in which people do bad things are so terrible that we could hardly expect them to do any better than they did. So we soften our judgment on them.

But even if we disagree on whether we should excuse a certain person for doing a certain wrong, or how much of the wrong we should excuse, most of us agree that people are sometimes excusable for doing bad things. If we do not excuse people we read about in the newspaper, we tend to excuse them if they turn out to be us.

Notice that when we excuse someone we do almost the reverse of what we do when we forgive that person. We forgive people only when we blame them. We excuse them when we decide we cannot blame them.

IS IT PERMISSIBLE?

Most of the debates we have about morality today focus on whether certain things are morally permissible.

Our doubts are peppered with questions like "May we? Is it all right if we do this? Does God allow it? Would our conscience feel right?" In short, our questions of right or wrong usually have to do with what sorts of things are permissible. Morally permissible, that is.

Is a woman morally permitted to have an abortion if she knows that her fetus has Tay-Sachs disease? Is it permissible to transplant a baboon's heart into a baby's body? Is it permissible to make nuclear weapons that can destroy civilization? Are we permitted to remove a machine that keeps a comatose person alive? These are all questions about what we are permitted to do.

We also ask whether we are ever permitted to do things that violate a moral rule that we all live by. Is it permissible to tell a lie if somebody's life depends on it? Is it permissible to steal bread if you are poor and your family needs to eat? Is it permissible to kill someone who attacks your spouse? Do circumstances ever make it permissible to do what the moral rules we live by tell us not do?

When we say that something is permissible, we are not giving it a four-star rating on the "rightness scale." We are not show-casing it. We are dealing with the lowest denominator of morality.

It is something like getting to first base on a fielder's error. If I hit a ground ball and the shortstop bobbles it, I am permitted to take first base. But I am not likely to get a standing ovation, and I do not even improve my batting average. All I get is permission to go to first base.

But my being on first base could be crucial to the ball game, so it is important for everybody to agree that I am permitted to be there.

It is that way with morality too. When we wonder whether we are permitted to let our aged father die or to have an abortion, we are usually walking on the edge of the meaning of our lives. We are talking about whether our humanity is being undermined.

Most things we do every day are permissible, and it never enters our minds to wonder about them. We don't usually need to ask whether we have moral permission to eat the kinds of food we eat, drive the kind of car we drive, enjoy our friends or make rapturous love to our spouses, or do most any of the normal things we do. Life would be a crushing chore, not to say a brutish bore, if we had to stop and wonder whether *everything* we do is permissible.

Some things are never permissible, of course, and we do not really need to wonder about them. Is anyone ever morally permitted to torture a child? Is it ever morally permissible to betray your parent or your country? Do we even need to ask?

IS IT TOLERABLE?

Every civilized group of people has to decide what it can tolerate. If a community tolerates everything, it commits social suicide. If it is so strict that it tolerates very little, it stifles individual freedom. So every group needs to keep asking whether certain types of actions ought to be tolerated.

When we do decide that a given action—gambling, let's say, or showing X-rated movies—is tolerable, we do not mean that it is morally good. Indeed, most of us believe that making and selling pornography is morally outrageous. When we tolerate it, we only decide that we shall not prevent other people from doing what we think is wrong. So some things may be morally impermissible and yet be socially tolerable.

On the other hand, when we decide not to tolerate a certain action, we do not necessarily mean that it is morally wrong. We do not tolerate people walking naked down Main Street at high noon. But this does not mean that noonday nudity is morally wrong; it only means that most of us do not want to see it on our streets.

Some people believe that society should tolerate things that— in their opinion—are morally wrong because they believe that all responsible people should be free to decide for themselves. That is, they believe we have a moral duty to respect individual freedom, and this belief counts for more than their belief that it is morally wrong to print hard-core pornography, let us say, or drink hard liquor.

In any case, when we ask whether a thing is tolerable, we are not asking whether it is morally right. We are only asking whether the rest of us can put up with it.

## IS IT OBLIGATORY?

When something is obligatory, we do not have any options. We have to do it, and we are in the wrong if we sit on our hands and do nothing.

When I am permitted to do something, I usually do no wrong if I choose not to do it. Permission to do it is also permission not to do it. But when I am obligated, I am not permitted not to do it. There is no choice.

The trick is to know the difference between what we are obligated to do and what we are only permitted to do.

When it comes to specifics, we are mostly obligated *not* to do things. We are, for instance, obligated to keep our hands off other people's throats and out of their pockets.

But the moral absolutes are always positive. We are obligated to be fair, and we are obligated to do things that help our neighbors. Justice and love are positive obligations.

If we think about it, even negative rules carry positive obligations up their sleeves. For instance, the rule against sleeping with someone else's wife or husband is a negative implication of the positive law of creative faithfulness. The rule against lying is the visible tip of a deep law that calls us to be lovingly truthful in all our relationships. The rule against killing people is the negative reverberation from a law of life that obligates us to help people live. Every moral "no" is the echo of a moral "yes."

In any case, when we say that a person is obligated to do something, we are going a step beyond saying that it is right for him or her to do it. If you have permission, you are free and clear if you choose not to do something. You may have permission to smoke a cigar, vote Republican or Democrat, and pull the plug on Aunt Sophie's life support system; but you are not thereby obligated to do it. But if we are obligated to tell the truth to each other, to pay fair wages to people who work for us, and to help starving children get something to eat, then we are at fault, in the wrong, if we fail to do these things.

IS IT EXCELLENT?

Now we have reached the summit of all rightness. We are not talking anymore about what we are permitted to do. Or even obligated to do. We move above mere right and wrong. We are talking about what is better and best. Maybe we are talking about style and class. Or the superlative works of love. The bottom line is excellence.

It is *moral* excellence that we have in mind.

But moral excellence has a lot to do with style. And skill. And finesse.

The fact is that good people can be morally clumsy, and botch the good things they do; and bungling can spoil morality.

I know of a Christian woman who does her duty by helping people a lot. She is very rich, and she does not have all that much to do, so she drops in on families in her village where the going has been hard, and she always leaves a gift of money. But she gives her gift with the deftness of a donkey. And always with a subtle hint that a little extra prayer and maybe a smidgin more ambition would get the family on top of things again. Nobody ever feels better for her coming.

I have a hunch that as much harm is done in the world by

good people who do good things poorly than by bad people who do bad things well.

My favorite ethicist, James Gustafson, recalls a night during World War II when he was sitting at a table in cafe having a drink with a friend. A soldier was sitting at the bar, two sheets to the wind, but ordering one more beer before he hit the road. He gave the bartender a twenty dollar bill and got six dollars in change—about thirteen dollars short.

Gustafson's friend saw what happened. He got up, motioned the bartender over to the side so no one else would hear what he had to say. He told him that he had seen him shortchange the drunk soldier and he also whispered in the barkeep's ear that if he did not slip the rest of the change to the soldier, the owner of the bar would hear about it.

The bartender meekly came across with the money.

Next, our man called a cab. He got the soldier's address from his billfold, and wrote it down on a piece of paper to give to the cab driver. And then he wrote a note to the soldier explaining what had happened, along with his own name and phone number, and pinned the note to the soldier's shirt pocket. The cab arrived, and he helped the soldier gently into the back seat.

But he did more.

He paid the cab driver enough to get the soldier back to his base. And before he let the cab drive off, he took the driver's number, just in case the soldier woke up the next morning and missed his wallet. Then, but only then, he sent the cab off.

He went back to his table, sat down, finished his own drink, and probably thought sadly about rotten wars that turn innocent boys into pigeons for venal barkeeps. And hardly anyone in the cafe noticed the moral drama played out before their eyes.

Moral excellence! We may not be able to define it, but we know it when we see it. Once in a while good morals become high art.

But there is more to moral excellence than doing good things in splendid style.

People also achieve moral excellence when they do more than any person is reasonably obligated to do. They move beyond the morality of "live and let live," beyond the Ten Commandments, into the excellence of unselfish love or unexpected courage.

Think of Rosa Parks, dead tired after working all day at some white folk's house, getting on a bus and plunking herself down in the white folk's seat, and staying there, not budging for all the white folk's power, and in staying put got a movement going that led the way to better times for white and black folks both.

Think of an ordinary straight-laced father, the sort of man who gets on his high horse and charges at every moral lapse he sees in our society. Think of him sticking with his drug-addicted son until the end when his son died of an overdose. Then, drowning in guilt and tempted to take his own life, he rallied his courage to live and devoted the rest of his life to helping other parents cope with children strung out on dope.

Think of Mother Teresa tenderly holding the head of a dying outcaste in Calcutta.

But think of yourself, too, at any moment in your life when you did something for someone, did it with no hope of a payoff, did it at some cost, did it only because that person needed you.

Think of such things and you will not need a definition of moral excellence to know it when you see it.

Now and then we make moral judgments, not to decide whether we are permitted to do the sorts of things we are doing; sometimes we simply see moral goodness, and we praise it, we see moral excellence and we celebrate it.


The human moral symphony has many movements. We make moral judgments, not simply as carping critics humped against the forward flanks of moral evil, but as children of God who want life to be truly and fully human, in all its features, as it was meant to be by its Creator. So we want to correct our course when we fail, and we want to celebrate when we do superbly well.

# CHAPTER 3

# Face the Facts

The facts, please. What are the facts?

We have to know the facts of the case if we want the privilege of having an opinion about it. If we do not begin with the facts, we are settling for make-believe.

Sometimes the raw facts are simply hard to uncover, maybe because somebody is hiding them, probably because the situation surrounding them is terribly complex. Try getting the facts, sometime, about the nuclear arms race. Or even about a family fight.

But knowing the facts as they really are is hard even when we all have the same data in front of our noses. The brute facts are there, but they are not the same facts for everyone involved.

Each of us sets the facts into his or her own picture of reality. The data speak different languages to different people. So when I say that the first job in morality is to know the facts, I am not making life easier for us.

We all filter our most significant facts through our personal beliefs, our feelings, our fears, our desires, and our values. And it is only after we filter our facts that we identify them as "the facts of the case." But by this time we have given each of them a subtle new shape, and we have given each of them the meaning we believe it has. The brute facts have become personalized facts.

Nobody has exactly the same set of beliefs and values inside his or her heart that anyone else has. So the filtered facts take on as many colors and shapes as there are people who look at them.

Enough reason, then, to consider some very important facts about facts.

## ONLY SOME FACTS ARE RELEVANT

Some facts have a bearing on whether an act is right or wrong, others do not matter. And some facts count for more than other facts do. One of the most important things we can do in deciding whether something is right or wrong is to make sure we know which of the many facts in any case really have a bearing, really count, really make a difference, or, in other words, which facts are relevant.

When we talk about moral absolutes detached from real life, we do not have to bother our heads about the facts of the case. For instance, we can say it is always wrong to cause innocent people to die. That is all there is to it. No point in sorting through a closet full of facts to find the relevant ones. We know what is right without looking.

It is when we come down from the mountain of moral principle into the side streets of reality that we have to separate the relevant facts from the irrelevant ones.

Ask whether it was right for Jack Palozzi to do something that resulted in Norma Walvoord's death, and you need to sift for the relevant facts.

The facts are these: Jack is Norma's doctor, and he has Norma hooked up to a respirator, which is the only thing that is keeping her alive. She is in a deep coma; Jack is sure she will never wake up, no matter how long they keep her breathing. Her brain is so badly damaged that even if she should surprise everyone and wake up from her coma she is not likely to be able to recognize her own children.

Jack removed Norma from her respirator. The result? She died within a few hours.

Now try to sift the relevant facts from the irrelevant facts, the facts that matter from the facts that don't matter. Norma was female, poor, widowed, Protestant: are these facts relevant? Of course not, you say. Another fact: she was eighty-five years old. Is this fact relevant? We are getting warm. Her brain is badly damaged, all but dead, registering next to zero on an encephalogram. Is this fact relevant? Yes, it must be. So some facts are more relevant than others.

How we tag facts as relevant or irrelevant depends a lot on what we believe to be really important about human life.

Sometimes the same fact becomes more relevant in one person's case than in another person

Take a fact like Alzheimer's disease.

Wes and Selma Kirkgraf had their thirtieth wedding anniversary in 1985. They have had the sort of marriage that a lot of people only dream about. They sailed together, they hiked together, they traveled together and, above all, loved together. But at her anniversary Selma was oblivious of anything that happened in thirty years of happiness with Wes. In fact, she did not know who Wes was.

Selma has had Alzheimer's disease for five years.

Wes has devoted his every hour to taking care of his dear Selma, grieved to despair as he watched her slip from a vivacious beauty into a helpless infant. Caring for her, he has let his business go down the drain; the price has been high, but, for Wes, worth every cent. But his children, grown, out of the house, have been worried about Wes's own health. He was becoming a hermit, depressed, grim, joyless.

"You have to go out once in a while," his son told him, "and be with some old friends, have some real relationships, forget things at home for an evening." Wes did, and does. On Saturday afternoons, down at the marina where he and Selma used to finish an early afternoon of sailing, he began to renew some old friendships, have dinner, dance a while, and enjoy a drink or two with a few single women he used to know. Lately he has centered his social revival on one woman, ten years younger than he is, divorced, an old friend of Selma's. He tells Selma everything, but she can only stare, her blank eyes fixed on a point somewhere in the past of a life lost to nature's whimsical harshness.

Sam's children tell him he is doing the right thing. Of course, their mother's sad condition is what makes it right in their eyes. Sam wasn't so sure to begin with; and even now he sometimes feels a little shabby. But he goes on because he is afraid he will surrender to his own sorrow and die inside if he does not keep some intimate touch with vital people.

Selma's blank mind and his own urgent needs are the only relevant matters.

What the neighbors think is not relevant. Not to Sam. Not even the fact that he is married to Selma is very relevant to him.

As Sam feels it, he and his wife are medically divorced. When it comes down to it, for Sam, the only relevant facts in his case are Selma's disease and his deep needs.

Harry Wilcut's wife Fern had Alzheimer's disease, too. She was a mewling infant at seventy-five, no more able to sit up and eat or go to the toilet than a month-old baby. Harry had watched her decay for five wracking years; now he felt in the depths of his heart that Fern's life was long gone. The real Fern, the woman who had filled Harry's life to overflowing, was dead, and what remained was a mocking ghost, a phantom whose blank visage was death's living insult to the person Fern was. He knew that Fern would rather be truly dead than falsely alive.

Harry shot Fern in the head. For her sake, he released her from the devil's prison and set her free.

To Harry, the fact that Fern had Alzheimer's disease was utterly relevant; in his eyes, what he did was tragically but honestly justified by it.

Not so, declared his judge. Alzheimer's disease may be relevant to many things. But it is not relevant to murder. Killing an innocent and helpless human being is murder, and no disease justifies it.

The same fact about different people. But that one sad fact is not as relevant in one case as it is in the other.

It is also true that a fact about one person that is relevant in one situation may be irrelevant in another situation.

Take Lucy Smother for example. She is white, single, forty years old, very smart, and for the past year, the vice-president of Asbury College. Phil Lubbers is black, married, with five children, sixty years old, and, for the past fifteen years, a night watchman at Asbury College. The school's board voted to raise Smother's salary by ten thousand dollars from fifty thousand to sixty thousand dollars a year. It voted at the same meeting to raise Lubber's salary by two thousand dollars from eighteen to twenty thousand.

Lubbers got a lawyer from the NAACP and argued that he was the victim of both age and racial discrimination. He was getting on in age, still had to educate five children, and he had earned a right to have his special needs considered when it came to a raise in pay. His seniority was relevant, he believed, and so was his need.

The president of the board believed that the only relevant

facts, the only facts that counted, were the facts that Smother was a vice-president and Lubbers was a night watchman.

One evening at five, Smother and Lubbers were standing in line at the checkout counter of a busy supermarket. Lubbers was third in line. Smother was tenth. Smother walked up to Lubbers and asked him to trade places in line. After all, she hinted, vice-presidents come first. But Lubbers did not flinch. The fact that you are a vice-president may count for a lot of money at the college, but it does not get you a step ahead in the checkout line. Vice-presidency at a college is not a relevant fact in the world of supermarket checkout counters.

How we decide which facts have a bearing on a case depends a great deal on the time and place we live in.

Take the case of Sally Rorf and Jim Geld. Sally is a manager of a branch bank. She does the same work, with the same competence, as Jim does over at another branch. But she earns three thousand dollars less per year than Jim earns.

She complained to the president of the bank, who reminded her that after all, Jim was a man, and that, as a woman, she was lucky to have gotten the manager's job at all. Sally hit the ceiling. "Any fool knows," she yelled, "that a person's gender is not relevant to how much he or she should earn."

Most of us today would agree with her. But would your grandfather have agreed? Probably not. Why not? Was he less moral than you are? Or did he just happen to live at a time when people were not awake to the irrelevance of a person's gender when it came to wages?

Once Jesus came upon some men ready to execute a woman who had been caught in an act of adultery. As far as we know, in those times a male was never taken in for adultery and certainly was never executed for it. Married men slept with other women and nobody cared very much. Married women who slept with other men became candidates for capital punishment. A man's maleness made it excusable for him to commit adultery and a woman's femaleness made it inexcusable for her. Then Jesus came and dared any man who claimed innocence to throw the first stone. No one took his dare, and the woman went home free. The difference between him and the lynch mob was that he saw no relevant difference between male and female when it came to casting blame for adultery.

Someone once said that all moral questions boil down to the

question of which facts are relevant in each case. An exaggeration? Maybe. But it is surely clear that when we make moral judgments, we need to know more than the facts; we need to determine which facts are truly relevant to what is being decided.

## ALL FACTS ARE INTERPRETED FACTS

Once we get them inside our heads, we begin interpreting the facts of a case. They do not stay brute facts very long. They become facts with meaning.

For instance, a man draws a pistol and shoots another man. The brute facts are that one man shoots a gun and another man is dead. But what do they mean?

We learn that one of the men was running away from a liquor store. He had just robbed the store and had shot and wounded the storekeeper. The storekeeper grabbed a handgun from his drawer and managed to shoot the robber before he got out of range.

But there is more. We listen to the storekeeper long enough to learn that this was the third time in a month he had been robbed. Each time the police showed up too late to help. And the robber got away. The storekeeper had decided that the only way he could protect his store and his life was to get a gun and use it to protect himself if necessary. Now we begin to understand what was really going on.

We interpret the facts, not by looking at a picture of a man with a smoking pistol, but by learning what his intentions were, what had provoked him, what had been going on beforehand, and what sort of man he was.

The one thing we need most when we interpret facts is a clear view of what they mean within the story in which they came to life.

This is never more true than when we interpret facts within our own experiences.

Everything, at least every important thing that happens to us, is a snippet in our continued story, the life story we are writing with our choices. Every episode in our story becomes the raw material for the next episode. And what we write next depends on how we interpret the previous chapter.

How we interpret the facts in our own experiences depends on whether we see our lives as continued stories or as disconnected episodes. Is my story a bunch of loose links that never form a chain, a collection of short stories that never get to be a novel? Or is my life a single story, with a beginning and an ending, and with all the odd little episodes making their special offerings to what is really a story line with meaning? How I interpret the details depends on how I understand the whole plot.

In any case, we always interpret the facts when we see them as parts of a larger story. And we make responsible judgments about the right and wrong of our choices only if we are willing to take the time, keep our cool, and ask how the facts fit into the story.

## FACTS ARE FELT FACTS

We feel facts as we interpret them. And we interpret them as we feel them.

The daughter of an alcoholic father feels differently about the fact of three-martini lunches than does a man who makes important deals at cocktail parties.

A black man making his living by working alone in Johannesburg, separated by law from his wife and children, feels the fact of apartheid in South Africa differently from the way his white bosses feel it.

The same facts become absolutely different facts in the feelings of two different people.

Two women are talking about a young assistant minister in their church who has come out of the closet and let his people know that he is gay. One of the women is a monumentally moral person whose children are settled down in successful marriages and fine careers, all happily heterosexual. The other woman has a son whom she loves more than life itself, the apple of her eye, a young man who earned, cum laude, a doctor's degree in English literature and is just beginning his career at a state college near home, and who told her five years ago that he is thoroughly, unchangeably gay.

Both women are trying to digest what they consider to be

the shocking fact that the assistant minister of their church is a homosexual person. One fact. Two feelings about it.

What difference does the way we feel facts make about the rightness and wrongness of things?

It makes a lot of difference. But the difference it makes cuts two ways.

On one hand, we all need to get above our feelings about things when we make moral choices—and when we form opinions about other people's choices. We are all tempted to shunt reason to a sidetrack and let our feelings take over. The stronger we feel, the more we let our feelings substitute for thinking. If it nauseates us, we condemn it without further thought. But nausea is not morality, and feeling sick is not a ground for moral judgment.

On the other hand, if we do not feel strongly about bad things, we may be neutralized, lukewarm, indifferent. And indifferent people do not care enough to make responsible choices. Many of us lived out years of our lives without a single strong feeling about racial discrimination. As long as our feelings were not aroused, we were incapable of understanding the deep curse that is racial injustice. So we could not evaluate it clearly, and we could not make good choices as to what we should do about it. Some things have to be felt in order to be understood.

Let me sum up what I have just been saying. Feelings have a powerful, but double-edged influence in our rational moral thinking. On one hand, strong feelings can blind us to the real meaning of facts, trip us into bad choices, and push us into unfair moral judgments. On the other hand, if we do not feel strongly about things, we often miss their moral meaning.

One more factor in our feelings about moral issues: when we feel very passionately about facts, we can easily forget that other people may feel strongly about them too. For this reason, the stronger we feel about things, the more important it is for us to listen to what other people tell us about their feelings.

If I remember that your experiences shape your feelings and that your feelings shape the facts you "know," I will listen to you patiently so that I can imagine what the facts feel like to you. And if I remember that my own feelings shape my understanding of the facts, I will try to let you know what my feelings are.

And I will remember how hard it is for us both to feel the facts as other people feel them.

To repeat: all facts are felt facts. If we keep this fact about facts in mind, we will be quicker to accept the fallibility of our own moral choices and slower to assume that people who disagree with us are wrong-headed or evil.

## ALL FACTS ARE EVALUATED FACTS

We all evaluate the facts we know. We not only "know" them as facts we can juggle and put into a computer; we also put them on a value scale and weigh them. We look them over, size them up, and put a price on them.

We evaluate facts in terms of how important they are. Some things are more important than other things. In every human situation where somebody has to make a decision, there are gut issues and there are peripheral issues. Some factors lie at the core and matter a lot. Some factors are at the surface and do not matter much.

For a spouse, saving his or her partner's life is more important than the high cost of surgery. For an accountant, account accuracy is more important than tax savings to his or her clients. For Martin Luther King, Jr., gaining justice for his people was more important than obeying segregation laws. For a corporate executive, the quality of his or her product is more important than the bottom line of this quarter's profit. When we settle on which things matter most and which matter least, we are evaluating the facts.

We either invest the facts on hand with value, or we divest them of value whenever we make moral decisions. And it helps to remember that other people give the same set of facts a different value than the value we give it.

Most great debates about complicated moral issues center on the differences in our values. We disagree about the morality of what is going on because we esteem things differently.

As a member of a hospital ethics committee, I once took part in an urgent discussion about whether to perform a risky operation on a very sick newborn baby.

The baby's parents were young immigrants from a tiny rural

village in Mexico. They both came from families of ten children, all of whom worked on the small family farm. The baby's doctor was a white Los Angeles specialist who knew nothing about life on a family farm in Mexico.

The baby needed an operation to survive. Besides other serious defects, he had Down's syndrome. So one fact in the case was that the baby would be mentally handicapped. Was it an important fact to consider in deciding whether to operate? It depended on how much value we place on mentally normal children.

What did the doctor think? Yes, he thought the fact of Down's syndrome was important and should be considered in the case. Why did a Los Angeles doctor think that the fact of Down's syndrome might count against performing risky surgery to keep this baby alive?

Well, American doctors tend to value intelligence very highly; they are likely to think that it is very important for any child to be mentally healthy, at least healthy enough to make his or her way in the modern world, maybe healthy enough to become a big city doctor.

What did the parents think? No, they did not think the fact that their baby had Down's syndrome was important and they did not think it should count in deciding whether or not to operate on their child. Why did they think that their child's Down's syndrome did not matter?

Simple. For a farm family in Mexico, in an area where all the children worked on the farm and all the farming was done by hand, a Down's syndrome child is an advantage. Children with Down's syndrome can be trained to do simple but all-important chores on the farm; they work gladly and productively without dreaming of the day when they can leave the farm and head for a better life in El Norte. So for these parents Down's syndrome did not count against keeping their child alive.

The American city doctor and the Mexican country couple put a very different value on the fact of Down's syndrome. And their differing values led them to different opinions on the choice between operating or not operating to try to save the life of a very sick baby.

All of us bring our values into any serious problem. If we remember this, we will have a better chance to understand each other's points of view. And we will be willing to compare our own evaluations of facts with the way others evaluate the same facts.

More important, we will be honest with ourselves about the price we really do put on things. We will test our real price against the price we advertise to our friends. Is there a gap between what we say our price is and what we would really sell for in the crunch?

The first step into responsible moral thinking is to be aware of this elementary rule: we cannot tell right from wrong unless we know the facts in the case.

We need to see them for ourselves, but we also need to know how other people see them. And we can get to know how other people see the facts only as we listen to them when they tell us what they see.

When we patiently listen to each other, and learn how the other person sees, interprets, feels, and values the facts, we discover facts are never mere facts.

People who have eyes to see and ears to hear, just as we do, see and hear the same facts as we do, but they hear a different message from the one we hear and they see a reality that is different from ours. If we really want the whole truth, we will let other people tell us why they see what we don't see and why they hear what we don't hear. If we listen to each other while we look at the facts, we may, together, get closer to reality than we could on our own.

Never trust the moral judgments of Lone Rangers.

To make right choices, we need to listen to each other as we reason together. We need to really listen, listen honestly—with a real desire to hear—listen with respect, listen with empathy, and listen with a humble sense of our own fallibility.

Be warned: genuine listening is risky. If we listen, really listen, we may adjust our own vision of the facts, we may revise our sense of their relevance, qualify our interpretation of them, modulate our feelings about them, and modify our evaluation of them. But the truth about the facts is that if we look at them through our eyes alone, we may miss their meanings, and if we look at them with other people, people we respect, we have that much better chance of seeing them right—and a much better chance, too, of making good choices when we decide what to do about them.

CHAPTER 4

# Respect the Rules

How do we know what is right?

One way to know is to follow the rules.

Obey the rule that fits your case. When you have to make a hard choice, and you are not sure you will make the right one, you will most likely do the right thing if you consult the rules, pick the one that applies to your case and do what the rule tells you to do.

There is a lot to be said for going by the rules. Rules make life easier and safer. They take some of the hassle out of morality; if we know the rules, we do not have to thrash out all the "yes, buts" and "on the other hands" every time we have to make a decision. With rules we know for sure, and we know ahead of time.

When we go by the rules, we know beforehand that we should keep our promises, and that we ought not to take something that belongs to someone else. And we know a lot of other things besides.

We are like a relief pitcher in baseball who thinks ahead— before he is called into the game—and knows what pitches he should throw to each hitter in different situations; he does not have to do his thinking on the mound when he faces the league's leading hitter. Or, we are like a quarterback who enters the football game with plays that he knows ahead of time are right for specific situations; he doesn't have to improvise every step along the way.

Moral rules are not fetters to bind us into moral straitjackets and steal our freedom. Nor do they take all the risks out of making choices or relieve us of the agony of making decisions when we are not sure which one is right.

Rules help us to use our freedom wisely. And they do reduce the risks. But we neither lose our freedom nor avoid risks when we accept moral rules as pointers to right choices.

Suppose you are an American tourist, driving on a country road somewhere in southern Italy late at night. You are looking for a little village few people have heard about. You have never been there before, so you don't have much to go on.

What you do have is a road map you got from the Italian Auto Club in Rome, and you have the good sense to follow it.

Would the map rob you of the fun of driving; would it be a bureaucrat's nasty tactic for killing the pleasure of cruising the open country? If you used the map, would you lose all your freedom or would you feel all the more free precisely because, with a map in hand, you could explore whatever promising side road struck your traveler's fancy without worrying about losing your way?

Would your map, on the other hand, relieve you of having to make real decisions on the way? Would you never have to wonder whether a certain thin black line on the map stood for the narrow road you just passed? Every American who has driven in Europe knows that even with the best of maps, you still have to make decisions you are not sure of.

In short, your map would free you to improvise and yet would sometimes leave you wondering whether you made the right turn when you hung a left at the last crossing.

Compare your trip on the sinuous southern Italy roads to the journey we are all taking through unmarked human situations we have never been in before and where we have to make hard decisions we have never made before. And compare the Italian road map to a tested set of moral rules.

Moral rules give us the same sort of help in deciding what to do in all the strange situations of modern life that a road map gives any driver trying to make his way along the twisting country roads of a foreign place. Our world has become a strange country to us, in many ways. And some reliable guidelines come in handy.

On the other hand, I have not yet found a set of moral rules that would relieve us of all personal responsibility for thinking and struggling and praying for wisdom in today's labyrinthian complexity.

In sum, moral rules neither take away our freedom nor relieve us of freedom's risks.

Moral rules are not inflexible fibers that bind us to convention and custom. Nor are there enough of them to cover every situation; we are often left on our own to use whatever common sense and responsible freedom we have at our command when we have to make hard choices in strange new situations.

So much for fending off conventional biases against moral rules.

Now, before we talk about how to *use* the rules, we need to understand what moral rules are. Not what they tell us to do, but only the sort of things they are.


## WHAT IS A MORAL RULE?

A MORAL RULE IS A STATEMENT THAT TELLS US WHAT WE OUGHT TO DO.

Or what we ought not do. It's as simple as that. Moral rules give direction. They prescribe; they do not describe.

True, sometimes we say that people do things "as a rule" when we describe what they usually do.

Dutch people, as a rule, have tolerated a dizzying range of opinions in their country. Marathon runners, as a rule, do not smoke cigarettes. The word "rule" in these cases is like the word "law" in the "law of averages"; it does not tell us what ought to happen, but only what is likely to happen in view of what has usually happened before.

Moral rules do not tell us what is likely, but what ought to happen. There are other words we could use instead of "rule," good words in their ways, words like "standard," "norm," "law," or "command." Each has a special texture of its own. But they are all like rules in this sense: They tell us what we ought to do and what we ought not do.

A MORAL RULE IS AN UNDERSTANDABLE STATEMENT.

Moral rules are intelligible. They are not secret signs, codes that only initiated members can decipher. They are ordinary sentences that anyone can understand.

A MORAL RULE IS A STATEMENT THAT TELLS US ALL WHAT WE
OUGHT TO DO.

Moral rules are meant for everyone. They are meant for all
of us simply because we are members of the human family.

Rules are different from commands in this respect. Commands are not for everyone in general. When a sergeant barks
a command at a private soldier, he expects only that particular
soldier to jump. But when someone says, "We ought to keep
our promises," he or she is repeating a rule that applies to everyone who makes a promise.

Of course, some commands are personal ways of pointing
out general rules to specific people. If I tell my son, "Come now,
tell Daddy the truth," I am only telling him to do what everybody
ought to do.

A MORAL RULE IS A STATEMENT THAT TELLS US AHEAD OF TIME
WHAT TO DO.

We can carry a moral rule in our heads and apply it whenever
we enter a situation that calls for a decision. We do not have to
wait until we actually get into a crisis, as if every situation is so
special that no rule could fit more than one. We know ahead of
time that it is wrong to kill an innocent person, wrong to sleep
with another person's spouse, wrong to steal a purse or a wallet,
wrong to let hungry people starve, and wrong to betray a friend.
The rules tell us in advance; we don't always have to wait and
see.

A MORAL RULE IS A STATEMENT THAT TELLS US WHETHER
SOMETHING WE HAVE ALREADY DONE WAS RIGHT OR WRONG.

A moral rule is a standard for taking the moral measure of
what someone has done. It not only guides us in choices we
need to make tomorrow; it tells us about the right or wrong of
choices we made yesterday. So a moral rule is both a directive
for the future and a measure of the past.

Enough, then, of what a moral rule is.

Now we must answer two major questions about rules.
Where do the rules come from? And how do they rank among
themselves?

Not all rules come from the same source.

And it makes a whopping difference where a rule comes

from. A crucial difference, at that. It could determine whether a rule has the rank of a moral absolute or the rank of a useful tip.

So let us talk, for the rest of this chapter, about the different *sources* of rules and about the different *ranks* of rules.


## WHERE THE RULES COME FROM

### THE RULES OF THE ORGANIZATION

An organization is a group of people who work (or play) together according to pre-set rules. Organizations cannot function without rules. And they cannot function effectively unless everybody trusts everybody else to stick to the rules.

In some organizations, rules can make a life or death difference. The surgical unit at General Hospital follows the strictest rules, and follows them with utter dedication. Inside the operating room these rules are unbending, critical, clear. Every doctor, every nurse, and every orderly knows what they are and how important it is for everyone to work by them.

But rules of the organization are not moral rules. They are rules that make for effective teamwork. Most of the time, a person is not morally in the wrong for violating them. Breaking the rule could cost someone his or her job, but need not make that person feel guilty.

An organization, in fact, could have morally bad rules; one, for instance, that required employees to spy and report on each other's private lives. Nobody in his or her right moral mind would consider it a moral virtue to obey such a rule. Or a moral failure to ignore it.

On the other hand, any organization may insert moral rules into its handbook because good morality sometimes makes for effective operation. Suppose your plant had this rule: "Everyone who borrows tools from the tool crib must return them." It would be a moral rule—"We ought not steal"—fixed into practical company policy. So you would be bound to obey it, not merely because the company issued the rule but because, in this case, the company rule is also a moral rule.

The conclusion is that an organization needs rules to get

things done efficiently, but its rules are not necessarily moral rules and they have only as much authority as their source.

We garner many rules from the storehouse of human wisdom. We learn by experience, and what this generation learns it passes to the next generation in the form of proverbs, maxims, and rules. Yesterday's lessons become today's wisdom. So if we follow the rules of prudence, we stand a fine chance of doing well, because the rules were distilled from the learning experience of people who came before us.

Prudential rules come to us by way of our culture's hoary customs. They are written in ancient books, like the biblical Proverbs. Or they come straight from our parents or teachers, who tell us to do what they tell us to do because they really know.

Rules of prudence tend to look like these: "Honesty is the best policy." "Women and children first." "Get a good night's sleep before you make an important decision." "Neither a lender nor a borrower be." "Never put off until tomorrow what you can do today." "Buy low, sell high." All rules of prudence.

Rules like these are "rules of thumb." All things being equal, we do well to follow them. But all things are not always equal. The sages of older days did not know everything. And they could not foresee many situations we encounter. Besides, every situation has something unique about it. So, if you find yourself in a situation where breaking the rules of wisdom is a more effective way of getting good things done, be our guest: break them in good health.

OPERATIONAL RULES

Everyone needs to make some personal rules to live by. Life is just too complicated for us to succeed at living it unless we make some rules for ourselves. Not many of us are morally smart enough to wait until we actually run into a crisis before we make up our minds about what we ought to do in such a situation. There are too many crises and too many temptations for us to cope well with all of them without a game plan. We need to make some rules for ourselves, in advance.

A doctor I know follows this personal rule: never perform an abortion. This is his own operational rule. He makes life easier for himself by following it. Therapists I know follow this rule: never cultivate social relationships with clients of the opposite sex. Parents make operational rules just to make life simpler for their young children. Most of us get through our complicated, seductive world more successfully when we follow at least a few operational rules that we make for ourselves.

But we need to keep the difference clear between the operational rules we make for ourselves and moral rules that obligate everybody. An operational rule for an alcoholic may need to be "Not one drink, ever." But the alcoholic does not necessarily insist that his or her operational rule is everyone else's moral rule.

## THE RULES OF THE CITY

Every city—or state—has to make rules (we call them laws or statutes) to spell out the limits of what it will tolerate. The trick is to have enough good rules to keep some justice, decency, and plain order alive in a society where different sorts of folk live together, but not so many rules as to whittle away their freedom. Too few rules bring chaos, too many of them stifle gladness.

The point I want to make here, however, is that a city's rules are not the same as moral rules. I suppose everyone knows this.

But the rules of the city and the rules of morality carry on a complicated relationship.

Most of the city's rules are echoes of moral rules. They restate moral rules that we already respect for moral reasons. Most people do not a need a civil law to tell them that it is wrong to embezzle money from a bank or to kill a neighbor because he plays his stereo too loudly. That is, some civil rules only put some bite into moral rules.

We all expect some moral rules to be translated into civil statutes. And for a simple reason. One person's moral wrong can result in another person's pain or loss.

But we do not agree about which moral rules should be turned into the city's rules, or which immoral acts should be treated as criminal acts.

Put too many moral rules into the city's books and you turn police officers into snoops. We don't want a cop peeking into our bedrooms or checking out the magazines we read. But if you get government out of morality altogether, society could become a cesspool, and children almost always get hurt when their society is a moral mess. There is a place somewhere between bluenosed Salem and everything-goes Sodom, and only good sense will tell us where it is.

In a pluralistic society, people do not all march to the same moral drumbeat. So we agree not to legislate every jot and tittle of morality or make all immorality a crime.

### THE RULES OF GOD AND NATURE

People who believe in God also believe that moral rules are God's rules. And that God's rules are also the rules of human nature. After all, if they are rules of the God who made us, they are naturally rules that fit who and what we are. We may get to know them via our conscience or via the Bible, but they come *from* God and therefore *are* the rules of human nature.

If an intelligent Creator made us, it stands to reason that he had a design for the sort of life he meant for us to live. So we should not be surprised if he furnished us with some instructions on how best to match our lives to his design. Or, in other words, how to bring out the best in our own selves.

His rules are user-friendly. Guides to humane living.

If the moral rules do in fact originate with our Creator, they are likely to have certain qualities that would be important to anyone looking for a liveable morality. If rules coming from God are at the same time the rules of human nature, we can expect them to share certain qualities. Let me suggest a few.

### THEY MATCH THE SORTS OF PEOPLE WE ARE.

They are not whimsical commands that a hard-driving deity throws down from heaven to make life less fun for his frolicking children. They fit what we are; if we follow them we will function roughly the way our very nature inclines us to function. In short, what we ought to *do* matches what we are meant to *be*.

If a single set of moral rules fits all of us, we probably all share a human nature, all grow as parts of a single family tree with roots and branches stretching through all the cultures we have made and all the epochs we have survived.

Moral rules point us to where our basic inclinations lead us; moral rules are the mirrors of our most basic human tendencies.

If there is a moral rule that we should not kill another human being, that rule only echoes the moral voice of our own souls. Thus our truest natures push us and the moral rules point us toward the humanity our Maker intends for us.

As I said earlier, moral rules are user-friendly.

We have all lost a lot of moral energy, just as some of us have lost our moral map. And we have followed a lot of destructive inclinations alien to our true natures. But this is a failure in the way we have handled our lives; it is not a failure in the design.

### THEY ARE FOR EVERYONE.

Since moral rules come from the Creator of the human family, they are meant for everyone who belongs to that great family. They are not exclusive rules for special people.

God's moral rules are mirrors of how all his human creatures are meant to live. The point is of the essence. The Creator of humanity is not a tribal God and his rules are not tribal laws.

### THEY ARE INTELLIGIBLE.

Anyone can understand God's moral manual. He does not grunt his will. Or give hand signals that only initiated members can read. His rules come to rational people in rational form.

Though not all people believe that moral rules ultimately derive from God, they can hardly misunderstand them.

Take a sentence like "It is wrong to kill an innocent human being." Is this a dark and puzzling message that only insiders can decode? Does anyone have to sweat over the rule "Always keep your promises" as if it were the riddle of the Sphinx?

### NOT ALL OF GOD'S RULES ARE MORAL RULES.

It is one thing to believe that moral rules ultimately come from God. It is another thing to suppose that all rules coming from God are moral rules. God has a stake in more things than morality.

There are rules for religion, for instance.

Morality is about doing right things. Religion is about being forgiven for the wrong things we have done. The rules of morality tell us how to live well with each other. The rules of religion tell us how to live well with God.

When we say that religious rules are about our life with God and moral rules about our life with each other, we do not mean that morality goes no deeper than human relationships. God no doubt feels very strongly about morality. Morality is rooted in God, and immorality can ruin our friendship with him. It is just that the word "morality" is the word we keep for talking about right and wrong among ourselves.

We all live by rules, but the rules we live by come from many sources. Where they come from says a lot about how serious we need to be about keeping them. If they come from human sources, their authority is limited and conditional, and the more authority is claimed for them, the more we need to keep a critical eye on them. When anyone says, "These are the rules, period, no question allowed," it is time to get suspicious.

## HOW RULES RANK

People who decide moral questions by moral rules eventually discover that not all rules have the same rank.

Some rules are absolute. They roll like moral thunder through the ages, down the hills of every civilization, and into the valleys of every culture. They hold all peoples everywhere to account, all classes, all creeds, rich or poor, ancient or modern. They come with an imperious claim to respect, everywhere, under all circumstances, in every nook and cranny of every individual's private or public existence.

Other rules are almost absolute. All of us ought to follow them almost all of the time. Extenuating circumstances may warrant our breaking them from time to time. But even then, people who break them have to demonstrate (at least to themselves) that they could not do right unless they broke the rule, and that their exception underscores the rule.

Still other rules are more like practical maxims for at least surviving, or doing well—maybe excellently—in a disorderly world. They are valid as long as we can make life a little better for people if we keep them.

Yet they touch some of the most sensitive moral zones in the human community.

They tell us things like how to spend and how to share our money. How to work and how to spend our leisure time. How to live and love in a sexual revolution. How to dress appropriately. And how to know when to stand back and let a very sick person die.

If we are brought up under rules covering such things, we tend to feel them as if they were the rules of God. But, as we begin to think about life a little more deeply, we wonder how undeviatingly they are really meant to be followed.

Almost all of us who have lived for a while remember rules we lived by once that are not rules we follow anymore. And some of us live by rules now that we put no stock in a while ago.

But where does all this leave us when we meet up with a specific rule? How do we know whether it is absolute, almost absolute, or relative? How do we know whether we ought to follow it no matter what or whether we should sometimes ignore the rule and just do what seems best for everybody involved?

The rules we find in the Bible leave us with the same questions. What a bewildering variety of rules we uncover there. The Bible does not label its rules with names like "Absolute Rules," "Almost Absolute Rules," or "Rules Only for the Time Being." How, then, do we know which rules in the Bible are meant for all people all of the time and which rules were meant for some people in biblical times?

To answer this question I will take my cue from the sorts of rules we follow when we play competitive games. How we play games tells us a lot about how we live together. And it gives us important clues to living by rules without being slaves of rules.

We all play games by rules. If we don't agree to follow the rules, we spoil the game for everyone.

Some rules we play our games by are more fundamental than others. Some rules we are never supposed to break. Others we can break now and then without anyone minding. The trick is to know *which* rules we may break sometimes and *when* we are free to break them.

There are, if you think about it, four sorts of rules for games we play. I will just list them here, and then we can compare each of them with the moral rules we live by.

Rules of Every Game

Rules of a Particular Game
Rules of Strategy
Rules of Propriety

RULES OF EVERY GAME

There are a few rules, not many, that we simply have to obey in every game we play. No matter what sort of game it is, no matter who plays it, or where.

Try this one, for example: we ought always to play fair. We've got to play the game in such a way that everyone who plays has a fair chance of winning; the only advantage that anyone may have over other players is the advantage of his skill or good luck.

Here's another example: we ought to play the game the best we can. If we don't play to win, we ruin the game. When my son was small, I used to let him beat me now and then at table tennis; but when I let him win, I was not playing the game, I was only making believe that I was playing. Later, when he was able to beat me, he never let me win; he really played the game. Winning may not be everything, but *trying* to win is the name of every game.

No matter which game we play—tennis or tiddlywinks, baseball or bridge—we ruin the game if we do not play fair and if we do not play to win. These are absolute rules that make or break any game.

Are there *rules of every game*, absolutes, for ordinary people in the serious game of life—the marriage game, the family game, the business game, the political game, and the many other games we play, all of them involving significant relationships with people?

Are there not at least two of them, and are they not the most important rules we could possibly live by?

One of them is a carbon copy of the first rule of every game: be fair. The rule of justice! The other is, care for people who need you. The rule of love!

Take the rule of love first.

The rule of love goes something like this: always try to help people who need you. Here we have the rule that makes every human game playable in a human sort of way. Where love is lost, humanity is lost, and all our human associations become bloodless combats where aggressive egos manipulate each other.

No wonder Jesus taught that the rule of love is the hinge for every other moral rule to swing on: all morality turns on love. Nothing is enough without love.

But love alone is not enough.

Suppose your family was a rollicking carnival of love. But it was all haphazard. Helter-skelter. When the mood was on. Your parents never called a halt to anything; they never said no. You got as much of anything as your greedy little heart desired, as long as the supply lasted. But some of the kids always got more than others, not because they needed more, but only because they got there first. I think you would agree: a love that never says no is a love that soon becomes unfair. And it usually ends up hurting somebody who gets the short end of it.

Love without fairness is almost as bad as no love at all.

So consider the rule of justice.

The rule of justice simply requires us to see that everyone involved gets a fair deal. The classic way of saying it is that we all ought to get what we truly deserve. To each his or her own: this is justice. No matter what association we are involved in— marriage, family, politics, corporation, or friendship—we ought to be fair.

Moses told the ancient Hebrews as they got ready to inhabit the promised land: "Justice and only justice shall you follow . . ." And the prophets echoed the rule across the landscape for hundreds of years. Amos's passionate summons was typical: "Let justice roll down like waters, and righteousness like a mighty stream." Nothing is enough without justice.

But justice alone is not enough.

Suppose your family specialized in fairness. And suppose the best thing you could say about your parents was that they always tried to be fair. They played no emotional favorites: all the kids were left equally far out in the cold. Perfect equality. You were all starved for affection at a table full of fairness. Never a good-night kiss, a long warm hug, a sigh that told you they really cared when you were hurt. With a family like this, you know that people need more than justice.

Love and justice need each other the way our skeletons need flesh and the way our flesh needs a skeleton.

We will feel the symbiosis if we recall the following ancient tale.

Jesus told a short story that has probably taught more people about real love than any story ever told. It is about a member of a minority group, a Samaritan, a salesman maybe, on a business trip to the city of Jericho. On his way he saw a man who had been mugged and left to die, bleeding in the ditch. Two other men, both of them religious teachers, had seen him too, but they were behind schedule on their divine missions, and they passed the poor fellow by. But the Samaritan stopped, personally bound the stranger's wounds, and paid a night's lodging for him at an inn before he went on; late, probably, for his appointment in Jericho. Chances are he lost a sizeable order for Judean figs.

The story illustrates that the rule of love asks us to help people, even strangers, who need us even if it costs us something, and that what love wants is *action* and not just a lot of talk.

But suppose there had been *three* wounded men on the road instead of one, and suppose the Good Samaritan had money enough for only one of them? The rule of love would have said, "You must help." But the rule of justice would have piped in, "You need to be fair when you help people." So make sure your love is fair when you choose which person to help.

Love tells us to care. But love works in a world of limited energy and limited money. You need a rule of justice to tell you whom to care for first, whom to care for most, and whom to leave to care for themselves.

In any case, there are two moral absolutes, they follow us into every nook and cranny of our lives and, whatever game we are playing, whatever relationship we are in, they pin us down with the dual demand: help people who need your help, but be fair whatever you do. These are absolute, they give us no escape hatches: everyone, always, in every human relationship, ought to have a heart to be helpful and a mind to be fair.

The ancient prophet Micah gave the people rules for every game: "What does the Lord require of you but to do justice, and to love kindness, and to walk humbly with your God?"

RULES OF PARTICULAR GAMES

Every game has its own basic set of rules. These are the rules that make it the special game that it is. Change the rules and you change the game. Allow players to break these rules whenever they feel like it and you will have a different kind of game than you had before.

Take baseball, for instance. One of the rules that makes it the game of baseball, as we know it, is that if a batter gets three strikes against him in a single trip to the plate, he is out. Now suppose a rookie was up against a cagey old screwball pitcher for the first time. Suppose he took a third strike, and then turned around to ask the umpire for another crack at it, a fourth strike, because he wasn't used to hitting screwballs and he really needed the job. The umpire would say something like this: "Are you pulling my leg, kid? Get out of here before I throw you out of the game."

Or take golf. A rule that makes golf the exquisitely frustrating game it is requires you to play the ball where it lies. Where it *lies*, mind you, not where you can get a clean swing.

Absolutely? Almost.

No exceptions? Hardly any.

If you take a third strike in baseball and the catcher drops the ball, you may make a run for first base. You will hardly ever get there before the catcher pegs the ball to the first baseman. But if you ever do, you can take first base legally even if you get three strikes against you.

If you drive a golf ball and it lands behind an artificial obstruction, you can move your ball the length of your club. Let's say a working crew went away the night before and left a small pile of drainpipes right next to the fifth green, and your second shot rolled snug behind a pipe. In that case, you would be allowed to move your ball. Play the ball where it lies, you say? Yes, except in rare circumstances where it would be unfair to ask you to obey the rule.

The serious games we play in real life also have their own basic rules, and these rules virtually make each game the particular kind of game it is. Rules that are all but absolute, because they are the rules that keep our relationships human. But still, rules you may sidestep under certain very unusual circumstances.

Take communication—the game we play whenever two or more of us share what is on our minds. One rule is fundamental:

do not deceive people. If you lead people to believe that you are
on the level with them, you must let them know what is really
on your mind. Honesty is a rule of the game.

Honesty, of course, is a matter of intention. We all make mistakes; but making mistakes does not make liars of us. And, as
we all know, we can deceive people with the facts. The rule is
that when we communicate with people we must intend to let
them know what we think or what we believe or what we feel.

If we don't live by this rule, we simply stop communicating.
Maybe we can still be persuasive. Sell junk to the gullible. Se-
duce the suckers. Manipulate the masses. But communicate? No.
Not if we ignore the rule of honesty.

Another game of life with its own special rule is marriage.

Marriage has one rule that makes it the special sort of relationship it is: the rule of fidelity. Two people follow the rule
when they share their lives in an exclusive partnership.

If both partners choose to agree to ignore the rule of fidelity,
they change marriage and turn it into something else. Whatever
relationship they make of it, what they have is not a marriage.
People are free, of course, to play a different game than marriage
if they want to. But then they should really give their game a
new name.

The game of property, too, has one basic rule: let people keep
the things that are really theirs. Change this rule and you change
the game.

If everyone took whatever he or she had a fancy for, no matter whose it was, we would no longer have property. If we are
going to play the game of property at all, private property or
public property, the rule of the game is, don't take what is not
yours.

Are rules of the game absolute? Almost. Not quite.

They are like the rule of golf that says, "Play the ball where
it lies." You must *always* play it where it lies. Unless! Unless some
unusual situation comes up that would make it unfair to ask you
to play your ball where it lies.

Take the game of communication once more, and the rule
against deception. If we don't agree on this rule, we simply give
up on real communication between each other.

And yet!

Suppose you had a secret. You knew something about a

friend of yours and what you knew could damage that friend, needlessly, if it ever became public knowledge. And suppose you made a pact with yourself never to tell a soul what you knew.

Now someone asks you point-blank, "Is it true that Jack was involved in a certain scandal back in the old country?" You are caught. If you say nothing, you will give Jack away. If you say, "It's none of your business," you will also give him away. But you don't have the wit to come up with a devious way to put your questioner off. So you make a choice: you tell a hard-boiled lie. You say, "No, it's not true." Or you tell a soft-boiled lie. You say, "I don't know." But it's a lie all the same, nothing else to call it; you really intended to deceive.

The truth of *this* matter is that the person who asked you to tell your secret about Jack had no right to that information. And the mere fact that he asked you the question did not give him the right to a true answer. Your only way to be true to your friend, and to your own promise, was to tell a straightforward sort of lie.

Take the game of property again; the rule of this game is the rule against stealing. But was it all right for the Dutch in Amsterdam to steal bicycle tires from the Nazis? Is it okay for a starving Cambodian to steal food from the invading Vietnamese army? Of course. In such cases stealing is the only way to gain back a little justice from oppressors.

If we only lived in a perfect world, we would never have to make exceptions to the rules of the game. But we do not have a perfect world. We have only this imperfect one, and it is the world we have to make our decisions in.

But the old slogan is still true: exceptions only underscore the rule.

Take this rule: we ought to drive within the speed limits. The limit on Fairview Avenue is 35 miles per hour. But your wife is in labor and in ten minutes is going to give birth to a baby, and you are driving her to the hospital at 60 mph down Fairview at two in the morning. A police officer stops you. You tell the cop what is going on, and instead of giving you a citation, he or she gives you an escort at 65 mph.

But the next day, the same cop is cruising Fairview, writing tickets. And no one is going to persuade this officer that the old limit is no longer in force just because you weren't given a ticket the night before.

Rules of the game are almost absolute. And in spite of the fact that we need to make exceptions to them once in a great while, they are still the directional signals that point our way to a truly human style of living, the kind of life we were meant to live.

### RULES OF STRATEGY

Every game we play has some rules for playing the game well. We call them *rules of strategy*.

They tell us things we have to do—or avoid—if we want to win. Or at least play the game well. Every person who plays a game splendidly can give you a pocketful of rules he or she plays and wins by. But that person is likely to add, "I am only telling you what works well for me."

You are allowed to break the rules of strategy whenever it suits you; no umpire will penalize you or even give you a dirty look.

Take baseball again. There is a rule of strategy that says, "Never intentionally walk the winning run." That is, never purposely allow a batter to reach first base if, should he score, his run would cost you the game. Managers obey this rule almost all of the time.

In football, one rule of strategy is, punt on the fourth down. In chess: always protect your queen. All rules for playing the game well.

But sometimes a baseball manager breaks the rule against intentionally walking the player who could score the winning run if he gets on base. Or a football coach may tell his quarterback to run with the ball on fourth down—if his team is desperate for a touchdown.

Smart players know the rules of strategy and they know when to break them.

The games of life have rules of strategy too.

Take the game of marriage again. There are strategies for turning a decent marriage into a happy one. It's not enough to keep the marriage intact by following the rule we call fidelity. It's not enough to be a faithful clod who turns marriage into a holy estate of tedium. What we need are rules of strategy for turning mere fidelity into creative fidelity, the kind that not only keeps people out of trouble, but moves them into the atmosphere of joy.

Or take communication. There are strategies for turning honest communication into interesting and helpful adventures in dialogue. It is not enough to cut and thrust through people's lives with honest meanness. Not enough either to bore our neighbors to death with truthful trivia. What we need are rules of strategy for communicating well, lovingly, caringly, helpfully. One such rule could be, "Keep your mouth shut and listen as honestly as you talk."

There is a story about Jesus that shows how he felt about rules of strategy. It happened that Jesus was taking a walk with his friends on a Sabbath afternoon and, getting a little hungry, they all picked some whole grain from a field and enjoyed munching it while they walked. Ancient rules of strategy did not allow Jews to pick grain on the Sabbath day. So some Pharisees scolded Jesus for doing it. But Jesus did not feel bound by their rules of strategy. He was ready to change the strategy if it made for a more humane life on the Sabbath.

For Jesus, the abiding laws were all about keeping life as human as possible. "The Sabbath was made for man," he said, "not man for the Sabbath." And rules of strategy are only devices to help us keep life as human as we can under the circumstances. When older rules of strategy don't work well anymore, we should drop them and make new ones.

My mother followed rules of strategy for Sabbath keeping. For instance, we knew ahead of time exactly what she would do on Saturday night. We did not have a bathtub at our house and we did not take baths on the Lord's Day. So she heated an outsized kettle of water on our big black coal-burning kitchen range, hauled a galvanized washtub out of the basement and set it in the center of the bathroom, poured the hot water into the tub, and oversaw the bathing of five grudging bodies.

Next she browned the sides of a pot roast, which she got for fifty cents, and gave it a head start for Sunday. Then she peeled her potatoes and scrubbed her vegetables, and set the dining room table for six, herself and the five of us kids. She did not make dinner from scratch on the Lord's Day. Finally, she saw to the polishing of five pairs of shoes; we did not put a brush to leather on the Sabbath.

All that on Saturday night after a hard day's work. We had not yet heard about weekends.

What was this Saturday night ritual all about? Did she think there was some divine law against taking baths and cooking dinner on the Lord's Day? I don't think so. My guess is that she was using rules of strategy, rules that worked for her so that she could clear the decks for a little peace and rest on the Sabbath day.

One day my mother bought a secondhand Roper, a white-enamelled, four-burner gas stove, with an automatic pilot light, and an oven she could set the temperature on. Sunday dinners were suddenly less of a hassle. So she stopped boiling the pot roast and cooking vegetables on Saturday night.

Then, on a marvelous day I still remember, a couple of men from Sears and Roebuck installed a porcelain tub in our bathroom. A year or so later they put in a water heater down in the basement next to the furnace. After that, when a few of us took a bath on Sunday morning, we did not violate the holy quietness of the Sabbath. I dare say that if somebody had invented an automatic shoe polisher, and we could have afforded one, we might have taken to shining our shoes on Sunday too; but we didn't.

Rules of strategy. Everybody who wants to live a serious life needs some of them. But they are not absolutes. We change them when things work well without them.

More important, we need to be constantly creating rules of strategy for ourselves. Like these, perhaps:

For the game of marriage: married couples ought to spend an hour of leisure time with each other every day.

For the protection of children: people who are sure that their neighbors are abusing their children should report their suspicions to the police.

For private property: we should put a ceiling on property taxes for retired people who have no income besides Social Security.

For communication: always make sure you have heard the question before you answer it.

Good rules, all of them, but only because and as long as they help us live well the life we ought to live.

## RULES OF PROPRIETY

Every competitive sport needs some *rules of propriety* to keep the game civil.

Rules of propriety are not fundamental to the game. We don't change the nature of the game when we break them. Besides, what is proper in one place blows the lid in another. What passes as proper manners for winter baseball in Mexico may unhinge an umpire at Yankee Stadium in June. But the game is the same in both places.

Some rules of propriety only make the game a little more pleasant to play; the rule in golf, for instance, that slow players should let faster ones play through, or the rule that the person who gets the best score on the last hole gets to tee off first at the next. Nothing crucial to the game here, just rules that give the game some of its special graces.

But some of these rules are terribly important to how the game is played. If a baseball player kicks sand at an umpire, he will be thrown out of the game. So what's a little dust on an umpire's blue pants? Ask any umpire. He knows it has to do with who is in charge and whether he can keep a game played by sassy millionaires under control.

Real life has countless rules of propriety. And some of them nibble at the fringes of serious morality. They get so close that it is sometimes hard to tell the difference between bad taste and bad morals.

And sometimes they affect each other. If we lose our sense of decency, we tend to lose our touch for the finer points of morality along with it. Vulgarity eventually dulls the sharp edge of our moral sense. Can we believe, for example, that constant exposure to film violence is only a threat to the public's taste for high art?

True, a person can be both vulgar and faithful, be a mite profane and still be honest, void of good taste and full of good morality. Better probably to be uncouthly moral than a classy louse. But over the long term, bad taste is more likely to corrupt good morals than fine taste is to change bad morals to good. So the ideal is to marry fine taste to good morals and let them live together.

The point is that rules of propriety, variable and inconstant as they are, deserve to be taken seriously; the trick is to respect them without promoting them to the rank of moral rules. Don't knock them, but don't absolutize them either.

The Bible has a lot of rules of propriety. Scattered around among the abiding moral rules of the Old Testament, for instance, we meet rules like this: "A woman shall not wear anything that pertains to a man, nor shall a man put on a woman's garment; for whoever does these things is an abomination to the Lord" (Deuteronomy 22:5). An *abomination* no less. It shows how deep decency cuts.

But what sort of dress "pertains to a man"? Every decent person in ancient Israel knew: the kind of garment suitable for a male was a flowing gown. Alexander the Great, on the other hand, knew that a real man on a military campaign wore a mini-skirt. And King Henry VIII knew that a royal male would blush if caught wearing anything but bloomers puffing over his support-hose. People have always "known" what sort of clothes a real male and a real female should wear. But from time to time and from place to place we revise our dogma of sartorial decency.

Our sense of propriety flows in and out with the tides of culture, and the rules change as our tastes change. But moral rules abide unchanging, ever challenging and ever confronting our personal moral inconstancy. A little moral savvy helps us tell the difference between them.

Now a quick look back.

Rules belong to life the way the scale belongs to music. And the way grammar belongs to writing. We cannot live the moral life without rules any more than we can make music without scales. Or write a story without grammar.

But not all rules are the same. Not even rules that guide our moral lives.

In the first place, rules do not all come from the same source. And it makes a lot of difference where the rule comes from. So the first question we discussed was "Whose rule is it anyway, and what difference does it make?"

In the second place, rules do not all have the same rank. And it makes a lot of difference what rank a rules has. We have looked at four different ranks a rule might have.

The Absolute Moral Rules, or the *Rules of Every Game*. There are only two of them: the rules of justice and love. They never change, and there are no exceptions to them, anywhere, anytime, for anybody.

The Abiding Moral Rules, or the *Rules of Particular Games*. These never change, and there are hardly any exceptions to them. We all play any game on the assumption that everybody who plays with us plays by the same rules we do. So we also move into every real-life situation on the assumption that we are going to play by the rules that govern that game of life.

The *Rules of Strategy*. These rules do change. They are relative, but a prudent person takes them very seriously. The less experience a person has at life, the more carefully he should follow these rules, if only because they come from people who have had success at living. But we cannot lay them on each other's conscience, and when it seems wise to break them, we can go ahead and break them without guilt.

The *Rules of Propriety*. These rules have to do with what is suitable and decent and fitting. They change gradually, and they differ from culture to culture. There are often exceptions to them, and they are relative. In some deeper sense of the word than we are used to, they have to do with taste. And it takes a discerning person, sometimes, to tell the difference between bad taste and bad morality. But there is a difference, and if we don't see it we can cause a lot of moral confusion.

What are moral rules for? They are signs that point us toward a good life. This is what rules are for: they tell us how to live in ways that contribute to the goodness of human life—our own and our neighbors'.

Rules are not sacred or even good in themselves. They are means, not ends. We are obligated by the rules because we ought to live the kind of life that ends in happiness for others and ourselves.

The point of view I have been expressing here is a version of what professionals call teleological, from *telos*, a Greek word that carries the notion of an *end* or a *goal* or a *purpose*; it is the view that morality and moral rules are really all about harmonizing our lives with the goal of the good and the happy humanity that the Creator dreamed for us.

Mind you, teleologists do not expect that following moral rules always brings instant pleasure. Sometimes it could cost us a lot of pain to do what a moral rule tells us to do. Nobody ever said that doing the right thing brings a terrific price in today's pleasure market. But in the long haul the road marked with moral rules is the one that leads to a world where being good and being happy are the same thing.

I think we are ready now to move on to the second way of knowing how to make the right choices. It is the way of results. It holds that you have made a right choice if the results are good. True? See for yourself.

# CHAPTER 5

# Consider the Consequences

Some people believe that the only way we can tell whether we have made a right choice is to consider what happened afterward. The test of right choices is results. It's as simple as that.

The theory goes roughly like this: if what we choose to do brings good results, we can be pretty sure that we are choosing the right thing. Or, if what we are thinking about doing is likely to produce good results, we can be reasonably sure we will be choosing the right thing to do.

The results do not have to be spectacular. They only have to be better than the results would have been if we had done something else. Or, if we are caught in a no-win situation, the results of what we do have to be less bad than the results of whatever else we could have done.

When we talk about good *results*, we mean that they are good *for* someone; we are talking about a good that touches real people and improves their chances of winning the struggle to bring a little goodness and joy into their lives. When we talk about some*thing* being good, we mean that it adds something good in real people's search for a good life.

If you are interested in a label for this point of view, it is usually called *utilitarianism*—the theory that right or wrong is tested by the utility of what we do.

What about using results as the test of right and wrong? Let me suggest two responses a person might give to this idea.

On one hand, anybody seriously interested in doing the right thing simply has to consider the results of what he or she does. After all, bringing good to real people's lives is what morality is all about.

Recall the two moral absolutes, justice and love. Why are these two things so crucial? Why are they unconditional and unequivocal, and why may we never compromise on them? When it comes right down to it, they are absolute because justice and love always secure human good, and any disregard for them always results in people getting hurt when it wasn't necessary for them to suffer.

Justice means being fair. And how can we tell whether we have been fair to people if we do not take into account how they are affected by what we do?

Love means being helpful. And how can we tell whether we have been helpful to people unless we know whether something good has happened to them as a result of what we did?

If you really want to be fair and if you really want to be loving to people, you have to let the results of your actions tell you whether, in real life, you are in fact being fair and loving for them.

Living right, morally, means living in ways that bring good things to people. And it means preventing bad things from happening to them. What really matters morally is whether we are adding to the goodness of people's lives. And for this reason alone, being moral means that we calculate the results of what we do before we can be sure that we are doing the right thing.

Results do count in the moral equation. It seems inhuman to suppose they wouldn't.

On the other hand, we cannot justify all our choices simply by adding up their results.

In the first place, some things are so bad that no good results could ever make them right.

I am talking here about good things that happen as a result of a bad thing someone does—good results he did not mean to bring about by his bad act.

Suppose a drunk driver hit and killed a four-year-old boy in your neighborhood. Would you and your neighbors not agree that this drunk did as bad a thing as any human being can do to a boy's parents? But suppose that through some surprising circumstances, good things actually happened to the boy's parents as a result of their tragedy. Could any good, any conceivable good, even great good, ever make it right for a drunk driver to kill their boy?

But good results do not justify bad things people do even though the people who do them have the best of intentions; good ends do not usually justify bad means. We don't give a blank check to well-meaning dreamers. We don't agree that doing great harm to real people is justified by dreams of great good for the masses of the future.

Does somebody's hope of improving people's material standard of living justify robbing them of their fundamental liberties? Would improving the human stock justify experimenting on sick babies? Would giving some of the profits to the Cerebral Palsy Foundation justify selling drugs to children?

If good results were all that count in the moral equation, we could justify any means to bring them about. But we would be fools indeed to live as if good ends justified any means. Some ends justify some means, but no end justifies every means.

Having said that not even very good results can justify every bad thing it takes to bring them about, we are ready to move on to the basic question: *how do we know which results are good?*

Who knows for sure what sorts of results are really good? How can we know unless we have a standard of reference?

Consider these questions, just for starters.

Do we really know *what* is good for people?

Do we really know *which* goods are better than other goods?

Do we really know *whose* good matters most, your good, my good, the majority's good, the poor people's good?

Do we know *when* people should get the good results, today, tomorrow, sometime later?

If you believe that you must be doing right because you are getting good results, you are assuming that you know what is good for people. Maybe you do. But are you sure you know what is good for me? Do I know what is good for you? Does the bureaucrat know what is good for all of us? Do we always know what is good for ourselves?

Maybe. Sometimes.

And *how* do we know? By adding up the results of what we do? Do we know what is good simply by counting how many cars we sold, how many houses we built, how much money we made, how many bottles of light beers we drank last year, how many unmarried mothers are on welfare, or how many nuclear warheads we have stashed away in Nevada? Of course not. We all know that counting things does not tell us a single thing about their moral quality.

If we know what is good for us—or anyone else—we know because we have sized things up, decided what they are worth, what we would pay for them in the currency of our sweat or our tears; in short, we have made value judgments about things. We have made some very important commitments, beforehand, about value, about what is really worth having and what is really worth keeping and what is really worth living or dying for.

We have decided whether it is more important to be free than to be comfortable, more important to keep our marriages together than to find fantastic love on the side, more important to be honest than to make a quick buck—and we have made a thousand other decisions about what is really good.

But sometimes we make our decisions about value before we really notice that we have made them. Some people wake up too late to reconsider the fact that they put too low a price tag on some things and too high a price on others. John De Lorean found out too late that he rated his integrity too low and his dream of producing a nifty sports car too high; but he put his price on these two things before he realized what his price was. And before he knew what was happening, he was ready to sell his integrity in order to keep his classy dream alive.

So we need to know why something is good for anyone, including ourselves, and we need to know how good it is before we can make good results the test of whether we are doing right. And to know these things we need a standard that we cannot get from results alone.

What we will do is this: we will look at the magic word "good" from several angles, keeping a sharp eye for hints as to what is really good—for whom. And when.

First of all, think for a moment about the word itself. "Good!" It is a catchall word for anything we approve of. A good book. A good person. A good idea. A good investment. A good God. You name it, if you like it you are likely to call it good.

The trick is to know whether what we like is really good. It is one thing to like something; it is another for it to be worth liking. Things are not good just because we like them, or even because a lot of people like them. We don't decide such things by a consumers' taste test. A thing is good because it is a thing of quality and because it does certain things well.

If you tell me you have a good watch, you probably mean that it keeps accurate time, the way a watch should. If I tell you that I heard a good concert, I probably mean that it entertained me with fine music superbly played, the way a concert should. But you compare your watch only with other watches. And I compare this concert only with other concerts. We don't compare your watch with my concert.

Another reason we call something good is to say that it is a sort of thing that all human beings do well to experience. But then we mean something different by its being good.

If we say that "love is good," we probably mean that among all the good and bad experiences people have in the world, love is one of the good sorts of experiences. To say that "love is good" is like saying "health is good" or "peace is good." There is something about all of these things that makes them good for us to experience them.

The world is filled with a fantastic, bewildering number of good things, like cows and children, stars and sonnets, families and freedom, birds and books, all sorts of things . Good things are so different from each other we wonder how in the world they can be enough alike for us to attach the adjective "good" to them all.

But, while countless things are good, some good things are better, in some ways, than other good things are, and one of the more splendid talents any serious person can have is the ability to sense which things are worth more and which are worth less. This will be the person who can tell what price he or she ought to pay for desired things. And, of course, when we speak of price, we are talking about more than dollars and cents.

So we end up with this question: what makes something good? Or, if two different things are both good, what makes one of them more valuable than other things?

## WHAT MAKES SOMETHING GOOD?

People who have thought about goodness a lot have come up with three reasons why we call things good:

A thing can be good for its own sake. (Call it an *intrinsic* good.)

A thing can be good because it is useful for making or getting something else that is good. (Call this an *instrumental* good.)

A thing can be good because it makes us better people to have it. (Call it a *moral* good.)

We can begin by asking what is good for its own sake. The first thing that comes to mind is happiness. So let's talk about happiness, about what it is and what we need to get it.

## HAPPINESS IS GOOD FOR ITS OWN SAKE

A few things, not many, are good for no reason at all. That is, we don't have to ask what they are good for. They are not good *for* anything. It is enough just to experience them. All we need do with these experiences is to celebrate them and be thankful.

Things good for their own sakes must be very good goods.

But what sort of thing is so good that we never need to ask, "What is it good *for*?"

Happiness is this sort of good. We don't want happiness so that we can use it to make a better living. Happiness is what we make a living for. We want things like health, or money, or friends because we believe they will help make us happy. But we want happiness only to be happy. Happiness is its own reason.

Ah, but what is happiness?

Everything depends on what we think happiness is.

Some people tell us that happiness is the same as pleasure.

Pleasure is a good thing, of course, a marvelous and wonderful thing. Can you imagine how unfailingly flat, how miserably monotonous life would be if we never scaled the peaks of pleasure? Or never even itched to do it? Hats off to pleasure! A million Stetsons off to pleasure!

But is pleasure what happiness is?

Take sensual pleasure, the pleasure we get from touching someone and having someone touch us, from savoring sweet sauces, from seeing striking shapes and flaming colors, and from hearing romantic music. What a sensational thing sensual pleasure is.

But is pleasure the equivalent of happiness?

Sensual pleasure is always limited; we get specific pleasures from specific things—a back scratch, a sunset, a glass of wine, physical love, all limited to one part of ourselves. But happiness is total; it lights up our whole selves, body and soul; it is the complete experience.

Not even emotional pleasure matches what we search for in happiness. It starts cooling off as soon as we get it. But happiness lasts.

Pleasure is never big enough, never lasts long enough, is not always noble enough to match the happiness fit for so uniquely God-like a creature as a human being. Pleasure is fine; we all crave it and some of us have unique talents for it, but it cannot measure up to all that we yearn for when we pray for happiness.

Aristotle described happiness as something like *wholeness*. We are happy, he thought, when our whole being is well—when we act well and when we are well, when we think well and when we feel well, when we are spiritually well and when we are well enough off materially to be comfortable. His notion of total happiness was called *eudaimonia*—"feeling well and being good."

It is this sort of happiness that we sometimes call "blessedness"—which is happiness with God at the core.

But what do we need for happiness? What is the recipe? What are the ingredients? Forget the bumper sticker definitions. Happiness is not a new kitten. And it is not being a grandmother. Not even winning a lottery. Happiness is made of many good things, a composite, a blend of goods from many sources.

Let us see if we can agree on some of the makings of happiness. I will list a few. Mind you, no one claims that any one of the ingredients by itself is enough to make a person happy. But it is hard to imagine anyone being truly happy if he or she misses out on very many of them. In any case, happiness requires a blend of things like these:

HEALTH

A happy person is a healthy person. We can hardly imagine a person suffering wracking pain and endless illness being happy. If he or she is happy anyway, it is in spite of the misery;

and there is probably a good supply of the other happiness makers present in his life. Sickness saps our happiness. Health feeds it.

## LOVE

A happy person is a loved person who knows he or she is loved. Can we be happy if there is no one in our life who names our name with love, no one who is glad that we are here, no one who feels sad when we are gone? For happiness we need to know we are loved and that we love someone in turn.

## FREEDOM

A happy person is a free person. I mean free in the sense that we can make our own pivotal decisions, the choices that steer our course in the mainstream of life. We have the inner freedom, the spiritual power, to become more of the person we know we are meant to be. Slavery does not mix with happiness, not in a soul meant to be free. Full happiness waits for free people.

## PEACE

A happy person is a person at peace. At peace in a lively singleness of spirit. He is one, single, clear within himself because he is at peace with his true self, his finest self, and with God. A happy person is not his own enemy, does not carry on endless war with his own soul. We may be fiercely at odds with the wrongs of the world around us. But inside our own selves, near the core, if we are happy we are at peace.

## TRUTH

A happy person is a person in touch with reality. Nobody can be truly happy in a world of lies or fantasy. Ignorance may be bliss, but it does not make for happiness. And how could we find happiness in deception? Happiness is being true to one's own self. Happiness is letting truth come into our thoughts. And happiness is the gift of speaking truly to others. Happiness needs the unfogged atmosphere of truth.

## BEAUTY

A happy person is a person who sees beauty. She drinks beauty, savors it, lingers over it, and comes back to taste it again.

Whatever is sordid, vile, or obscene blocks happiness. True enough, a person can walk in the alleys of ugliness and still seize the hem of the garment of happiness, but he or she will be happy only in spite of the ugliness. Happiness walks in beauty.

## CHARACTER

A happy person is a morally good person. Well disposed, at least, and on the way toward personal excellence. Can you conceive of a happy person who is evil? Happiness comes in the company of strong virtues; it comes with courage, not with cowardice, with honesty, not with humbug, with compassion, not with a stony heart.

Good people are not always completely happy. Not in this world. Not always. Being good could cost you some of the other ingredients of happiness. There are times when you could lose your freedom and even your life for being a good person. But you can be sure that total happiness, when it comes, will be holding the hand of a good character.

## GRATITUDE

A happy person is a grateful person. In fact, gratitude is the bottom line of happiness. If you have health, freedom, and beauty, but are not grateful for them, you are a miserable human being. No one can be happy while he or she is everlastingly grousing about life. A happy person is likely to be someone who knows that existence and everything that comes with it are gifts. Happiness is gratefulness.

There you have them, the makings of happiness: health, love, freedom, peace, beauty, truth, character, and gratitude. Add to them as you will. There may be more. But we can't get by with less.

Most of us get happiness here only in snippets, fragments, more or less and only now and then. Something is always getting in the way. But we do experience it for fragile moments that we are forever trying to recapture, and we keep longing for complete happiness only because we have tasted its promise.

Some of my readers may be surprised that I have not included God in my list of things we need for happiness.

Actually, a person's experience of God is the *core* of happiness. It is not just one more ingredient in the recipe; it is the heart pumping the warm blood of life into all the other things.

An experience of God has several dimensions, each of which is vital to our lasting happiness. When we experience God, we experience

The Creator who is the living source of our very being

The Savior who forgives all our failures

The Spirit who enables us to move toward wholeness, and who nudges us to hang on, by our fingernails sometimes, because we know that in the end happiness will win out over sadness and sorrow

These are the inner sources of the happiness we feel even when other segments of life get grim.

People sometimes talk as if they need only God in order to be happy. But the good news is that the Creator never meant us to have him only. Why else would he have made us so needy for friends and lovers? Why else would he have created us so ripe for sweet fruits and joyous sounds? Why else would he have given us eyes to look in beauty's face, ears to hear happy human voices, skin to feel the touches of affection? And why else would he have set us down in a world so filled with things we relish? He made us so that we could have all this and heaven too. Or, better, heaven, too, in the midst of all this.

God is generous enough to give us himself and his splendid gifts besides.

What bearing does all of this have on how we can know whether our actions are right or wrong?

Just this: if what you do brings about greater happiness for people, including yourself, there is a good chance that what you are doing is right.

Remember, we are not talking about pleasure. Giving people pleasure is not at all a sign that what you are doing is right, any more than it is a sign that you are doing wrong. But whatever we do that increases people's health, assures their freedom, creates beauty out of squalor, deepens their gratitude, and so on, is likely to be right.

But not all good things are good for their own sakes. Some things are good not for what they are but for what they can do for us. We call them instrumental goods because they are good instruments for producing more good.

## MOST THINGS ARE GOOD BECAUSE THEY ARE USEFUL

If somebody asks why something is good, we usually tell them what it is good *for*. Things are usually good because they help us get something else.

Money is good because it buys good things like food; only misers think money is good for its own sake. Knowledge is good because we can use it to make the world a better place; only elitists think knowledge is good for its own sake. And marriage is a good thing because it is the best way for people to express their love and makes the best environment for rearing children.

We can, of course, use good things for bad ends. We use money to manipulate people. We use food as a weapon to get people to do what we want them to do. We use knowledge to blackmail people with. And we use marriage to exploit the person we are married to. We can misuse almost every instrumental good as a tool for mischief.

But we still call things good if they are *meant* to serve a good end. And because we cannot get good things done without them.

On the face of it, we are doing the right thing if what we do helps people get instrumental goods. But it is not a sure sign that we are doing a right thing. It depends on whether they have a right to them, for one thing. Or need them, for another. And also on whether they can and actually will use them for the right ends.

When it comes down to it, we cannot be sure we are doing the right thing at all if our only proof is that we are helping people acquire instrumental goods. There are too many other factors involved.

## SOME THINGS ARE GOOD BECAUSE THEY MAKE PEOPLE GOOD

Most good things are simply nice to have. We are not better people for having them. And we don't deserve blame because we lack them. We may thank God for having them and we may complain because we don't. But we do not add to or diminish the excellence of our character either way.

Being healthy does not make you a good person anymore than being sick makes you a bad person. A gold medal Olympian may be a crook, and a leper may be a saint. Having money is no more a sign that you have a good character than being poor is a sign you have a bad one. Any millionaire can be a knave, and any pauper can be a moral giant. In fact, most good things put us morally on hold; it is good to have them, for sure, but you don't become a five-star character by getting a pile of them. This is why we call them nonmoral goods.

As I said, most good things are nonmoral goods. But nonmoral goods are terribly important to the goodness of human life. It is better not to be poor, not to be hungry, not to be sick, and not to be homeless, even if you can be a morally good person in spite of being poor or hungry or sick or homeless. And it is a good thing to have enough means to live well, to have food in your stomach, to be healthy, and to have a nice house to live in; these are good for people even though having them does not make people good.

If what you are doing adds to people's nonmoral good, there is a reasonable chance—all other things being equal, which they seldom are—that you are doing right. If what you are doing—or refusing to do—tends to deprive people of nonmoral goods that they need and have coming to them, the odds are that you are doing something wrong.

But let's talk about moral goods, the sorts of goods that make us better persons for having them. They are properties of the human spirit. If we have them and if we tend to live in ways that demonstrate them in action, we are on the way to personal excellence.

We used to call them virtues, qualities that make for excellence, sometimes greatness, but always goodness in people. Consider some examples: courage, compassion, fairness, loyalty, discernment, honesty, and modesty. Most people would consider anyone with a nice blend of qualities like these a good person.

What makes a person with qualities like these a good person? It is not because we enjoy being around courageous and fair people; they might be quite resistably unpleasant. It is not because honest and loyal people are especially amusing; in fact they might be depressingly dreary. We have no guarantee that moral goodness always comes with charm thrown in.

We say that these are moral qualities and that people who have them are good people because they are likely to make life better for others. You can depend on them to keep life human around them. To be there for you when you need them. To care about people getting a fair deal. To help people who need help. To respect your privacy when you want to be left alone. To let you know the truth when they talk to you. And to keep their hands out of your pockets.

The point is simply this: we call people good because they add to the goodness of other people's lives. Morality is always about keeping life good, or making it better, or preventing it from getting worse than it already is. This is why it is good to be a good person. Not so that you get God to applaud you. But so that you do some good for your friends and neighbors, even for your enemies.

Moral virtues are not the only good qualities worth having. It is good to be charming, and smart, and assertive. It is good, too, to be talented and imaginative, with a splendid streak of self-esteem thrown in. But you are not what we would call a good person just because you are lucky enough to possess these positive powers. Fortunate, yes. Good? Not necessarily.

How much credit anyone actually deserves for being a good person is hard to say. Most of our moral qualities are gifts of God. Or hand-me-downs from good parents and a good environment. So if we do have good characters, we have more reason to give thanks than to congratulate ourselves.

Still, there is something good about admitting—at least to ourselves—the virtues we find in ourselves, even if they nestle uneasily alongside some nasty little vices.

I was reared to pray that God would make me a good boy, but that I should never believe he answered my prayer. If I actually dared to claim that I was the least bit good, I would be guilty of pride. And pride is the worst sin of all. So I had to want badly to be good but never admit that I was.

I think now that we went too far with our humble beating of the chest. I have a self-esteeming hunch that I was not as bad as I felt like. And that if I had enjoyed the little virtue I had, God would not have clobbered me for the sin of hubris.

I think now that maybe people should simply admit that they are pretty good people as long as they feel grateful to God and other people for having helped them along the road. And as long as they don't kid themselves by overlooking the mean stuff sneaking through the back alleys of their souls.

In any case, it is good for a person to be good, because good people tend to make life better for other people.

So when we do things that help people become better people, we are doing right. Maybe even excellently.

We have been talking about the sorts of things we call good. If we believe that good results are the acid test of right action, we have to be able to recognize a good result when we see one. So we have been trying to get a bead on goodness.

What we have seen is that goodness comes in several shades. And shapes.

To recognize goodness in all its varieties, we need a standard of reference.

If you want to know whether you have an excellent diamond on your hands, you need to test the quality of the gem by some accepted standard of reference. In the same way, before we can let good results be the test of right and wrong, we need an accepted standard of what is good. And that standard of reference does not come from surveying the results of what we do. It comes from somewhere beyond that. And that is why we cannot know whether we did the right thing *simply* by checking out the results of what we did.

But even if we know goodness when we see it, we had better be aware that some good things are better than other good things. This fact, too, needs to be factored into morality. So let's talk about it.

## SOME GOODS ARE MORE IMPORTANT THAN OTHER GOODS

We ought to do the sorts of things that add to people's good. And, obviously, we should not do things that are likely to make their lives miserable. This is the essence of morality.

But some good things are more important for people to have than other goods are. And some evils are worse than other evils. Would we not agree that it is better to have good health than to have a big house? Worse to have cancer than to have migraine headaches? And better to have a brief but shining life than a long and wicked one?

It follows that when we have a choice between doing something that brings very good results and doing something that brings mediocre results, we should do what gives us the better results. And when we must make a choice between lesser evil or greater evil, we should choose to do the thing that results in a lesser evil. Elementary, you say.

But how do we know the difference?

Is it more important to be free than to be secure? Do you really think so? Is it more important to be courageous than to be clever? Is it more important to have peace and quiet than it is to have justice? To have nourishing food to eat than to have good movies to see? How do we know?

One way to answer this question is to see the difference between good things people *need* and good things people *want*.

THINGS PEOPLE NEED

Goodness knows, we all need a lot of things. And, offhand, as a rule of thumb, we could say that things we really need are more important than the things we desire. So ordinarily, we do right when we act to provide people with things they need.

But we do not all need the same things. At least, we do not all need the same things equally much. A handicapped child needs things at school that a healthy child does not need at all. A fully employed stevedore needs food different from the food a retired and leisurely person needs.

And, even more crucial, we all have different levels of need. Some needs may be more important than other needs.

It may help if we focus on a few of our need levels.

First, we have *survival* needs—the things we have got to have in order to exist as live human beings.

Second, we have *growth* needs—things we have to have in order to develop into more complete human beings.

Third, we have *freedom* needs—opportunities we need in order to determine our own lives as human beings.

All of us would agree that these are real needs; none of them
are luxuries that pampered people happen to hanker after. They
are what all of us need in order to manage life in a truly human
fashion.

Let's look at each need separately.

Take *survival* needs first.

We all need a certain amount of food and drink, air and shel-
ter, sometimes medicines, if only to keep body and soul together.
But we also need some love and care, someone to be with us,
to love us, accept us, touch us, forgive us; we need these spiritual goods if only to survive as living souls.

Even here we can see a difference. Some survival needs are
first-order needs; food is one of them. People who lack them just
a short while, die. Other survival needs are second-order needs;
loving attention is one. People who lack them slowly wither and
shrink, and finally die within themselves.

Then take *growth* needs.

Growth is of the essence for spiritual creatures like us; we
*need* to become more of what we are. When we stop growing,
we begin to die, even if we postpone our funerals for fifty years.

What do we need in order to grow? We need some knowledge, and so we need teachers and books and schools. We need
some wisdom, and so we need families, friends, counselors. We
need some touch with beauty, and so we need some green grass
and trees, some form of lively art, and some caring people
around us.

Growth needs are relative, even though they are real. Mary
has it in her to win a Nobel prize in mathematics; James can
hardly get through ninth-grade algebra. Their needs for special
math tutoring are not the same. Fred can become a first-class
violinist; Jean is tone-deaf. Fred needs a superior violin teacher
in order to grow, and Jean needs something else for her to grow
in her special way. And on and on through an infinite variety
of growth needs.

Yes, all of us have a deep need to keep growing toward whatever we can be. Growing is seeded into our humanity; our only
differences lie in the ways we grow and the things we need to

nourish us. Perhaps we can say this: Everyone has a need to grow as much as he or she is able to grow.

Finally, consider our *freedom* needs.

We all need some freedom to decide our own futures, to keep our own bodies free from other people's exploitation, to keep our own property free from the hands of anyone who would steal it, to maintain our privacy free from snoopers, and to live any place we choose and can afford to live. And we all need freedom to give thanks to God.

These are freedoms *from*—from what other people can do to fence us in or invade our space. They are the external freedoms; freedoms from intrusion and freedom from unfair constraint.

We also need freedom *for*—for doing whatever we believe is right and for becoming the people we ought to be. But no one else can give us this freedom or take it away from us. It comes from inside; it is freedom of the spirit, the inner power to become what we have the potential to become.

So much for human needs: survival needs, growth needs, and freedom needs. Most every need we have fits somewhere in these three categories.

But what do human needs have to do with the question of right or wrong? Just this: as a general rule, we do the right thing if what we do lets people keep or helps people get the things they really need. And we are doing a wrong thing if what we do tends to deprive people of things they really need.

We are not ready to say the same thing about desires. But before we say anything, we need to know the difference between what we desire and what we need. So let us talk about *desires*.

THINGS PEOPLE DESIRE

Nobody has an obligation to give people whatever they want. Benevolence does not require you to give me your Buick just because I would rather have your Buick than my Volkswagen. You don't have to be a fool even if you are generous.

We have to draw some lines between desires.

We can desire

Good things we really need
Good things we do not really need
Bad things that hurt people

So the mere fact that people desire things does not mean that we do right by providing them.

As a rule of thumb, we do right if what we do results in people getting things they desire *and* really need.

Good things that we want but do not really need are more iffy. If I help you get a Ph.D. degree, a free trip to Europe, or a slightly used Mercedes, I may be doing right. But not for sure. I could be doing a wrong thing if getting these goods for you is unfair to others who wanted the same good things and deserved them more than you do.

In any case, we are not *obligated* to provide people with things they want if they do not need them. Love obligates me to do things that help feed hungry people. But love does not obligate me to provide them with a microwave oven.

But people also want bad things. Here we never do wrong by saying no to a person's desires. I do no wrong if I ignore a drunk's desire for another bottle of booze or an addict's desire for another snort of cocaine or my children's desire for an extra hour of violent TV. But this hardly needs to be said.

How do we know whether people really need the things they want? Or whether things people wish for are helpful or destructive? We know only because we have a vision of what it means to be a human being. Of what human beings need in order to stay human or grow more human. And of the sorts of things that undermine their humanity and stunt their growth.

Now we will shift our focus. We will look not at results as such, but at the people who get them. If an act is right when it has good results, we must almost always ask, "For whom?"

## WHO SHOULD GET THE GOOD RESULTS?

None of us can help everybody, not even everybody who needs our help. We do not have enough good things to go around. Nor enough time and energy. So we have to choose the right people to help. Or, at least, the people we will help first.

Do I do right if I take care of my own needs first? Do I do right if I feed my children first and give poor children what mine have left over? Do poor people in my country come before poor people across the sea? Do the children of today get helped when helping them could deprive the children of tomorrow?

Think again about the Good Samaritan. If he had met three people lying half dead on the road to Jericho, and he had to make a choice, how would he have known which one to help? And which to leave to the luck of the highway?

Is there a general rule to tell us who comes first when, no matter what we do, we leave somebody out?

Consider two options:

*Everyone ought to do what is best for himself or herself.*
*Everyone ought to do what is best for the greatest number of people.*

Take the first one. According to this rule, it is your duty to look out for number one; take good care of yourself. This is what morality is all about: you are doing the right thing if what you do has good results for you.

Incidentally, we often call this point of view *egoistic utilitarianism*.

People who believe strongly in love, and love's penchant for thinking of the other person first, may wonder how decent people could build an ethic on selfishness.

But very decent people, in fact, *have* endorsed egoistic ethics, and have offered two main arguments to support it.

First, we all *do* look out for ourselves, and all our pious bromides about living the unselfish life cannot undo this fact about our deepest motivations. All our loving gestures have an egoistic hook. If we gave all that we own to feed poor folk, we would do it because we knew we would feel better for having done it. Different strokes for different folks; some people like to *feel* unselfish and other people like to feel rich. And they are all equally egoistic.

Therefore, since it is human to seek our own good first, it must be right to seek it first. So some philosophers have argued.

Second, if we all seek what is *truly* good for ourselves, we will all, almost naturally, be seeking what is good for others as well. The world is so nicely harmonized that if everyone looked after his or her own enlightened self-interest, it would work out best for everyone else too.

Are these two ideas true?

Is it true that we are always out to feather our own nests? Do we have a selfish motive for *everything* we do? When we wipe away another person's tears, are we only trying to make ourselves out to be tenderhearted folk? When we feed hungry people, are we only trying to justify our own full bellies? When we give a friend a gift, are we always trying to get something back from him or her? Don't we *ever* lift a hand to help other people, just for their sakes, without an eye on the payoff for ourselves?

But suppose we were all egoists at heart, would this mean that we have a *duty* to put ourselves first? It is one thing to admit that we are all selfish; it is another thing to build an ethic on that disappointing fact.

And is it true that if I concentrate only on my interests, and everyone else looks after only his or hers, we would all come out the better for it? What is the track record of unchecked, if enlightened self-seeking; does it produce a generous and a fair society?

If, then, it is a more generous ethic we want, we may consider the second option: we ought to do things that will result in the greatest good for the greatest number of people. Here the number of people is what matters most; the more people who enjoy good results from what we do, the more likely we are to be doing the right thing.

Most people have a soft spot in their hearts for a benevolent ethic like this.

How does it work? Simple. You calculate how much good you are likely to do for how many people. And then you compare this amount of good to any good that might have resulted had you done something else.

What counts is the *quantity* of results for a *quantity* of people.

Let's see whether it really works.

Suppose we could supply every single person in Burundi with a year's supply of Coca-Cola and a TV set for every hut in every village. A lot of good for a lot of people. But is it the *sort* of good that makes sense for hungry people? And suppose, besides, that we could not bring this great *quantity* of good to all those people without bribing a few officials along the way. Would the results really be worth the effort?

The example is crude, I know. But it does show that a large amount of good done for a large number of people is not a sure sign that we are doing the right thing.

Suppose, then, we brought a necessity like staple food to 70 percent of the people in a poor country. But then we discover that the 30 percent we did not feed were the hungriest and need-iest of all. Would we have done the right thing?

Here is a little story. It is often told to put the "greatest good for the greatest number" theory to a test. Try it for yourself.

Six spelunkers are exploring the belly of a cave. A sudden rock slide cuts them off from any exit. The rocks fall on one of the explorers. He is not dead; in fact he could last a couple of days, which is all it may take for rescuers to find him and dig him out. The other five can hear him and he can hear them.

A spring of water breaks loose in the rock slide and begins to pour into the small cavern where the other five men are trapped. The water will fill the cavern in a few hours. There is no escape. If nothing is done, the five will drown.

One of the five has some dynamite sticks with him. He figures they are enough to blow a passage through the rock pile. But he also figures that if they use the dynamite to save their five lives, they will kill the chap buried in the pile.

Five human lives to one. Should they destroy one life in order to save five lives? Are numbers the clincher?

Suppose you were one of the five and the man beneath the rocks were your son. Would numbers matter most then?

Suppose you were sure that the dynamite would kill the man buried, but you were not sure that it would blast a hole big enough for the five of you to crawl through?

Suppose one of the five said, "I only know that it is wrong to kill a person. Maybe if we just do what is right, and put away the dynamite, God will see to it that we are all rescued." What would you say to him?

Clearly, "the greatest good for the greatest number" does not tell us for sure that we have done the right thing. Sheer numbers are not convincing.

Again, we need rules of fairness and we need clear-cut values before we can evaluate the rightness of what we do by the amount of good things we bring to a large number of people.

There is one more question we need to face up to before we can make results the test of right and wrong. It is the question of *when* we should expect the results.

ARE QUICK RESULTS BETTER THAN SLOW RESULTS?

Now and then we have to chose between doing things that bring good results quickly and things that bring good results slowly.

We all know, of course, that *some* short-term pleasure is a lot worse than long-term tedium. Ask anyone with a loved one addicted to cocaine.

But the comparison is not always this stark.

Suppose you had to decide whether to allow farmers to use insecticides that brought a vastly improved harvest of vegetables to the market. Suppose also that the insecticides gradually filtered into the rivers and killed off several species of wildlife there. Worse, it eventually caused a slight risk of certain cancers among the consumers. Would you choose for the better harvest? Or would you choose to avoid risking the health and life of future generations of fish, birds, and children?

Suppose you chose to prohibit the insecticide. What would be the criterion you would use to test the rightness of your decision? Obviously it would not be merely the test of good results—because both decisions would have good results. It would not be the test of good results to the greater number of people—because more people would benefit from the use of the insecticide than would be harmed by it. Why, then, do you chose to reject instant benefits for the sake of avoiding long-term harm?

Could it be that you remembered an abiding moral rule that forbids killing innocent human life? And that it was this rule that formed your bias against big and instant benefits to a large number of people when those benefits carried a more important, if delayed, threat to human life in the same package?

One problem with making important decisions on the basis of long-term results is that what happens later is often out of our control. In fact, we can go for an undeniably good short-term result, succeed in getting it, only to have other people come along later and turn our decision into long-term disaster.

In 1944, Franklin D. Roosevelt went for a short-term result when he decided that the United States should make an atom bomb. The short-term results of his decision came in 1945 when the emperor of Japan surrendered on the deck of a United States aircraft carrier. But could Roosevelt have predicted what some irrational tyrant might do with nuclear weapons in 1994?

Can we know for sure what the long-term results will be now that we have given free reign to experiments with genetic engineering? Can we know for sure what a dictator with an evil mind might do in 2500 A.D. with the techniques we are developing today?

And we need to know what the odds are on securing the long-term results against abuse by bad people. We do not always know for sure. We make our decisions with the best understanding we have. Sometimes we make them in agony and with something less than the wisdom of the gods. But one thing is sure: we cannot go by results alone. We need rules to measure the results.

We have looked hard at most of the questions we face when we make the results of our actions the test of whether they are right or wrong.

I have hammered on the anvil of this theme: before we can use results to justify our actions, we need criteria for knowing what is good, what is better, what is bad, and what is worse.

We need

Standards to test whether the results really are good

Standards for comparing the value of different results, for telling which are good, better, or best, or maybe which are bad and which are worse

Standards for determining who should receive the good when there is not enough for everyone

Standards to determine when we should go for instant good and when we should choose postponed good

And where do we get the standards we need? This is the deepest question of all. Some of us feel no need to ask it, let alone answer it. We simply use the standards that filter spontaneously through our own humane feelings. We just know.

As for me, I need a faith that sheds light on what is good and what is right. I need a faith that tells me that the rules of justice and love are God's own absolutes, which are never up for grabs in anybody's world. And I need a faith, too, that assures me that we cannot substitute these two absolutes for anything, that goodness and decency will eventually break down when these rules are ignored. I need a faith that assures me that respect for human life, for truth, and for property produces better results for the most people in the long run.

Results matter, and they matter a lot. It would curdle the milk of human kindness if we steered our moral lives without keeping a kindly eye on how our acts touch the lives of other people.

We cannot live by moral rules alone, not in a broken world, a crazy world where to obey one rule can compel you to break another and where being right according to the rules can be wrong according to what it does to people.

We cannot live by results alone, either, not in a complex world where results that feel good today can go sour on us later, and where good results for some people bring disaster to others.

To live a successful moral life, we need to follow the rules while we keep a sharp eye on the results of what we do. But we can shift the sentence around and it would be just as true. To live a successful moral life, we need to keep a sharp eye on the results of what we do while we follow the moral rules.

But most of time we maneuver our ways through freedom zones where what matters is not whether we have done the right thing, but whether we acted wisely and well considering the options we had. There are huge areas in our lives where the question is not whether we did right or wrong, but only whether we acted like responsible people. This is the stuff of our next chapter.

# CHAPTER 6

# When You Can't Be Sure, Be Responsible

Most things we do are neither here nor there as far as right and wrong are concerned. They are neutral: they do not cut any moral ice at all. It is a right choice if you decide to do them and just as right if you choose to stay away from them.

When we decide whether to wear a blue suit or blue jeans, drive a Buick or ride a motorcycle, invest in mutual funds or real estate, be a plumber or be a doctor, we do not need to worry about doing the right thing—in the moral sense of the word. Morally, we are in a no-lose situation.

We could be wrong in a lot of other ways. Our choices could cost us money, lose us sleep, or make us look bad. But nobody can blame us as though we had done something morally wrong. We certainly need not feel guilty about them; a little dumb, perhaps, but not guilty.

Maybe 95 percent of our daily decisions are about things that do not matter one way or the other morally.

And yet, depending on conditions, almost anything we do can *become* morally important. It may not be wrong in itself, but we can do it in a wrong way, at the wrong time, in the wrong place, with the wrong people. A morally positive thing can become a moral negative when it hurts someone else. The *how* and the *when* and the *where* and the *why* can make the moral difference.

Think of driving on a crowded freeway for a whole day. There are a few rules that you have to drive by: keep within the speed limit, stay in the right lanes if you are pulling a trailer, don't drive while drinking alcohol, and the like. You ought to obey these rules, and so should everyone else on the road.

But during a day's driving you need to make hundreds of on-the-spot decisions that are not covered by rules. When to cut into traffic as you enter the freeway, what to do about the truck that is tailgating you, how to respond to the crazy driver cutting in front of you, when to stop for coffee. These are situations that no one can make rules for. At least not rules that fit everyone all the time.

You have to make your own rules of freeway strategy. And maybe some rules of freeway propriety. But you probably will change your rules sometimes, and break them too. And you will not expect every other driver to follow your rules exactly as you do.

For the most part, you decide what to do when the time comes. This does not mean that your spur-of-the-second decisions are not important. A lot of people are dead today because of legal things that freeway drivers did at the wrong time and in the wrong place.

There is a catchall rule for driving on the freeway that covers all situations—whether or not there is a traffic rule for them. The rule is, *drive responsibly*.

The moral side of life is this way, too.

We do not have to worry about breaking moral rules every time we turn around. Life can be light—and free. So why not take it in stride? Why overload the moral circuits? Life is more fun when we keep morality in its place.

The Greeks had a word for things that are neither here nor there morally; it was *adiaphora*—from a combination of words that come down to meaning "not at the heart of the matter." The *adiaphora* are out in the remote suburbs of morality.

The morality of the Ten Commandments is at the center where things really matter morally: if you kill innocent people, lie in order to take advantage of someone, sleep with someone else's spouse, or steal your neighbor's watch, you are aiming straight at the moral center. But when you chose what you wear, what you eat, where you live, how you amuse yourself, you are walking in the moral suburbs where being responsible is every bit as important as being right.

Remember that we can hurt people by doing right things irresponsibly. And we can hurt ourselves if we do things that are right for most people but are not good for us. There is a time and a season for all things, and sometimes the right thing at the wrong time can be worse than a wrong thing any time.

Like driving on the freeway, life's broad plains of freedom are covered by one broad law: *live responsibly*.

To live responsibly, we need to *be* responsible. Let me tell you what I mean by *being* responsible.

The American scholar H. Richard Niebuhr taught us that responsible people have three qualities:

1. They are able to initiate action.
2. They are able to make a genuine response to the situation they are in.
3. They are able to account for their actions.

Take a longer look at each of these qualities.

First, *responsible people initiate action*. They make decisions and these decisions set things in motion. And when they decide, and not until then, something happens.

Responsible people's choices are really their own, not all preset in a genetic code or predetermined by psychic fate. They do not *have* to do what they choose to do. So what happens as a result of their choice would not happen—at least it would not happen in the same way—if they had not chosen to do what they did.

The responsible person really does make things happen.

Second, *responsible people's actions are an answer to what is happening around them*.

Their actions are responses, not reactions.

They walk into every human situation wide awake to what that situation might ask for them. They assume that every new situation they enter is asking a simple question: "What will you do about me?" And every person is asking, "What will you do about me?"

Responsible people look for and interpret the signals coming from individuals around them. And they call the shots as problems arise. They try to understand what is going on, and then respond in a way that fits the question. Their actions are answers, responses, not reactions.

Third, *responsible people are willing to explain their answers*. They have reasons. They do not try to account for their acts by saying, "Well, I was in the mood," or "We have always done it this way." People are able to help other people see *why* the thing they did made sense in that situation, and can show why they thought their action was fitting. Responsible people don't need to argue that what they did was the only right thing to do. They only have to show that it was an appropriate thing to do in that situation.

So much for *being* a responsible person. You would have caught my drift if you were to conclude that being a responsible person is almost the same thing as being a moral person.

Now I want to talk about making responsible choices, about *acting* responsibly.

Mind you, when we talk about acting responsibly, we seldom deal with an either/or, as if we always had clear choices between doing something responsible and doing something irresponsible. Most things we do are more or less responsible. Life is not always pass or fail; it is mostly plus or minus.

So when we believe that we acted responsibly in a certain situation we might very well allow that someone else could have done something different in the same situation and also have acted responsibly.

Do you recall the different categories of morality that we discussed in the second chapter? The final one was the category of excellence. Only morally right things can be excellent. But to do a right thing excellently, you have to do it wisely and well, with fine timing, and maybe even with a bit of style. Responsible acts are likely to have a touch of class.

The fact is that people spoil morally right acts by doing them irresponsibly.

Take Irma Geldsma, a woman who prides herself on her uncorruptible honesty. She always tells the truth. But she tells truth that other people are much better off not hearing. She batters people with truth, cuts and slices into their souls with truth they do not need. Are you fat? Irma will make sure you know. Is your son on drugs? Irma will not rest until you know that her son just made Phi Beta Kappa. Did you share a secret with Irma? Count on it, she will tell anyone who asks her. Irma is an honest woman. But not being a responsible woman, she makes a vice out of her virtue.

At the other end of the spectrum, we can do bad things responsibly. And thereby limit their badness. Take a young man who makes his girlfriend pregnant. A classic case of wrong behavior. But suppose that when he learns that his girlfriend is pregnant he admits that he is as responsible as she is. Suppose, besides, that he offers to marry her, and suppose that he leaves college and gets a job so that he can support a pregnant wife. It seems to me that he cuts his moral losses a lot by accepting accountability. And he opens a door to a new beginning for his bride, his future child, and himself.

By acting responsibly in a bad situation, our young man turns his wrong into the start of something good. He does not convert a bad thing into a good thing. But he cuts his losses; by acting responsibly he limits the wrong he did by making it possible to bring a beautiful ending out of a bad beginning.

Acting responsibly, we can create good out of wrong things we do. Just as we can spoil a right act by doing good irresponsibly.

How do we know when we are acting responsibly?

Are there some marks of responsible behavior? Can we test ourselves for responsibilty?

I think we can test ourselves, but the only way to do it is to ask ourselves tough questions about our style, about our typical way of carrying on with people.

The tests have to be about *us*, about what goes on in our minds before we make our moves, about how we think, how we listen, how we feel before we act. Responsible *persons do* responsible things. So it helps to know if we *are* responsible people.

Are you up to testing yourself? Remember, we are testing the most important single feature of our character. Be encouraged, though, because we pass the first test of character if we are even willing to put ourselves in the dock.

I will put each test in the form of a question each of us can ask himself or herself.

## HAVE I USED DISCERNMENT?

In the words of a ballad Kenny Rogers used to sing about a card shark, "You've got to know when to hold 'em. You've got to know when to fold 'em. You've got to know when to walk away." The first test of responsible action is whether we have kept our eyes and ears open to what is going on. So that we will know when to "hold 'em" and know when to "fold 'em."

The name for this ability is *discernment*. We have it when we can be depended on to sense what is really going on around us and what is the better thing to do about it.

Some people always seem to notice things that other people miss; they catch little touches that are terribly important but seldom obvious to people who never look beneath the surface. They see subtle shifts in body language, hear delicate messages in other people's tones of voice, catch quiet hints that less sensitive people never notice. They have discernment.

They see the little things that make a certain movie great *before* they read the reviews. They know whether the book they are reading is an unusually good book even if it never becomes a best-seller. They can tell at a glance that you have rearranged your furniture. They have an eye for the details that make a difference.

They visit good friends and hear delicate signals that all is not well; so they guard their tongues, and say nothing that could make things worse. She senses that her husband is keeping something from her, that he is secretly sulking behind his usual grumpy exterior, and she soon catches faint hints that tell her he is having trouble at the job; so she makes sure that she does not blurt out something that could make him feel worse. He notices that his secretary's mascara is a little smudged, and senses that she has been crying, so he says nothing but makes sure he is ready to drop everything else should she want to talk about it.

Discernment separates the moral artist from the moral bungler. Bunglers know the rules but do not see what is going on in front of their eyes. They do not make good choices because they have not discerned what the situation calls for—the more helpful words, the more useful actions for *that* occasion.

If you are discerning, you take your time. You do not act until you catch an insight into what is going on in other people's feelings, into what is really on people's minds, into what people really need at the time. You wait, you check your impulse to shoot from the hip, you do nothing, say nothing, until you have gotten a good sense of what the situation really calls for.

If you are discerning, you can tell the difference between what is important and what does not matter much in a human crisis. You can tell the difference between things that need action now and things that can be put off until tomorrow, between people who need to be confronted and people who need to be comforted, between words that can be taken literally and words that disguise the real message a person wants us to hear.

If you are discerning, you can see the difference between quiet changes that make something truly new and showy changes that only spread cosmetics on a musty old surface. And when you discern whether you are facing a truly new situation or just a variation on the same old thing, you can tell when the moment has come for radical intervention and when the situation can be saved with a little prudent tinkering.

Discernment, not sheer intellect, not true grit, but simply being awake and having a nose for what is going on beneath the surfaces, and having a sense for the more fitting response to it—this is what makes for a class act on the moral stage. Discernment is the secret to living a creative and loving lifestyle with people we want to live with and have to work with; it is the key to making good choices when we are walking on paths where no one has posted signs to tell us where to go.

But, like everything else, discernment takes practice; it doesn't come easy. It is a gift, and like all personal gifts it comes only with exercise. It is not a gut reaction; it comes with using our eyes, our ears, our minds, our imagination, our empathy and, yes, our intuition.

We have to decide whether we really want to practice it. Or whether we want to go on jumping to answers before we have heard the questions.

We are all shoved and yanked around by our private schedules. And the more successful and busy we become, the better excuses we find for not taking time to see, to hear, to sense, to feel what is really going on when people get in our way.

Not many people reveal themselves on cue. They need time. What they want to say needs patient listening. And what they do needs interpretation. The discerning person gives them time to reveal themselves.

Doctors discern what is really going in their patients' lives when they take the time to establish personal relationships with them. Teachers discern what is really going on in their students' lives only if they try to see beneath the surface of behavior problems. Parents sense what is going on in their children's lives when they summon enough energy from their overtaxed hearts to listen long enough to hear and to look long enough to see what is actually going on behind the angry crackle of their adolescent hothead.

We do not fall into discernment by a lucky accident; we have it because we exercise it. And we often refuse to exercise it because we do not *want* to know what we might see if we used discernment.

We all edit out segments of reality that will cost us something to think about. We pay attention to what we really want to know. We prefabricate molds to fit our private reality into and we reject the parts of reality that do not fit our molds. We whittle and chisel reality into nice shapes that fit our needs. We abridge our consciousness to protect ourselves.

Our founding fathers declared that all people were created equal, but they screened out of their own consciousness the reality of thousands of black people living without freedom before their eyes. Pioneering Americans edited out of their minds the reality of Native Americans, their traditions, their national identity, their sacred rights to their own land, and their beauty as creatures of God. German citizens refused to discern the reality of Jewish people disappearing from their neighborhoods and villages, and thus refused to know that the Holocaust was happening just around the corner.

A suburban mother refuses to see the clear signs that her son is taking drugs; it would be too painful to let the reality inside her consciousness. A husband closes his eyes to subtle signals that his wife is having an affair; he refuses to know that he knows. Later on, he may say, "I really knew, but I did not want to know."

It is so hard, and it hurts so much, sometimes, to let reality inside our minds, to let it crash in full force when we want for all of God's good world to ignore it. Our sensitivity to pain can trick us into presorting reality, and let only the segments in that fit snugly and comfortably into our precast reality molds.

But when we abridge our consciousness, we cannot give genuine responses to what is really going on around us. For a simple reason: we don't see what is going on. Our actions become reactions. Not responses.

So one test, a very sensitive test, of whether we are making responsible choices is this: have I discerned what is going on around me?

Here are a few questions worth asking ourselves when we want to know whether we have used discernment.

Have I tried to hear what people are really saying to me; have I listened? And have I checked to make sure I heard what was being said and not what I wanted to hear? Or what I expected to hear?

Have I kept my cool? Or have I let my anger deafen me or my desires blind me?

Have I had enough empathy to put myself in the other person's shoes so that I could imagine what he or she was feeling?

Have I been honest with my own memory as I compared the present situation to similar situations of the past? Have I looked for ways in which the present situation is like others I have experienced before? And have I been flexible enough to see the ways in which the present situation is different from situations that I assumed were exactly like this one?

Have I paid unbiased attention to all that is going on; have I resisted the temptation to see only what I want to see?

In other words, have I used my gift of discernment?

## HAVE I INTERPRETED THE QUESTION?

Every situation that involves us asks a question: "What will you do about me?" And every decision we make is an answer to that question.

But a question needs to be interpreted. And we cannot really answer the question that our situation is asking unless we *interpret* it before we act.

There is almost always more going on around us than meets the eye. People talk to us, but there is more to what they are saying than a tape recorder can tell us. Things happen in front of our eyes, but there is always more to them than a videotape can tell us.

It is half past two on a Sunday morning. My daughter, Cathy, seventeen, out with the family car, was supposed to be back by midnight. I am out of bed, pacing the floor, worried sick, angry as a caged cat, when I hear the car's tires crunch the pebbled driveway. My daughter walks in the door. I pounce, with words heavy as thunder from the holy mountain—before she opens her mouth. I react to the fact: my daughter kept me out of my wits because she did not come home when she promised. The fact, yes, but the uninterpreted fact.

Later that morning I heard the interpretation. One of her friends had gotten into some serious trouble and needed help. Cathy did not feel she could let her friend down and she "knew" I would not understand if she phoned. So she risked my wrath and stayed with her friend. Maybe she was acting responsibly. I was not.

I acted irresponsibly; I did not give a genuinely human response to the question my daughter's action asked of me at half past two on a Sunday morning. I gave a reaction, not a response, simply because I did not listen long enough to interpret the brute facts of the case.

In 1961, the Soviet premier, Nikita Khruschev, decided to install offensive missiles on the island of Cuba. U.S. aerial photographs pinned down their identity; we knew the facts. Cuba, a hostile nation ninety miles from our shore, had missiles pointed at Boston, Detroit, Los Angeles, and any other city in between.

The facts thrust a question to President John F. Kennedy: "What are you going to do about us?"

The president brooded in the Oval Office, listened to his counselors, and tried to interpret the data. Certain military men seized on the plain fact that offensive missiles were poised ninety miles from our shore. And they reacted to this plain fact by saying we should send our bombers to destroy the missile sites now. Others wondered, "what does Kruschev have in mind? What are his real intentions with this mad move? How will he respond to our response? How should we interpret the facts?"

Kennedy interpreted the brute fact of missiles in our backyard in the light of everything he knew or could guess about Khruschev's thinking. He answered the question the missiles posed only after he interpreted the question. His answer came in the form of a decision to blockade the Cuban coast. And the Soviet premier answered, in turn, by dismantling his missiles.

The Soviet premier and the U.S. president looked at each other eyeball to eyeball and, in Dean Rusk's words, the Soviet blinked.

No one, I suppose, would claim that Kennedy's decision to blockade Cuba was the *only* right thing to do in that awesomely critical moment. Maybe there was a better answer that he could have given. There were certainly worse ones. But we can be sure of this: President Kennedy acted responsibly only because he *interpreted* the terrifying facts before he acted.

Some people see only what meets the eye and they react to what they see. Other people interpret what they see before they act.

Some people are slaves to a script; they always react the same way to crises—as if their reactions were predestined. If they fly off the handle, they say that they have no control over their tempers; someone else *makes* them angry, they never make themselves angry. They act as if every infuriating situation called for the same reaction.

Responsible people do not let prewritten scripts determine what they do; they truly respond to each situation, and they are able to give different responses as one situation differs from another. They know that the facts of any situation can be interpreted in different ways, and that they will act well only if they hold back on action until they get a reasonable interpretation of the question the situation is asking.

If you know that your situation is asking a question that calls for a response, and that the question needs to be interpreted, you are likely to act responsibly.

So, one test of whether our action was responsible or irresponsible is this: did we wait long enough to interpret the question?

## DID MY ACTION FIT THE SITUATION?

Some people have a natural sense for what is fitting. They always have the apt words to say to people who have just had some bad luck. They always bring suitable gifts that are just right for the occasion, not too showy or expensive, not too small or cheap. And they never mar anybody's party with stories that embarrass the guests. Some people have a knack for the appropriate.

Most of us have to stop and think, or ask someone who really knows, read a how-to book, maybe, or even hire a secretary. We have to work at it. Doing the fitting thing takes a lot of work for most of us, and even then we are seldom sure we did the right thing, or said the right thing.

Whether it comes naturally or whether we have to work at it, appropriateness is a test of whether we are acting responsibly because responsible action is action that fits the situation.

We are appropriate when what we do matches what the situation calls for.

If what you do is too much or too little, or just out of place, if it makes people uncomfortable, if it leaves everyone in the circle ill at ease, it is probably inappropriate. It may not be morally wrong; it might be quite all right if you did it another time and in another place. But in your place at the particular time, it didn't come off well because of your bad timing or clumsy choice of words.

We are talking about taste, certainly, and we are also talking about good judgment. A successful executive told me once that he hardly ever looks for job skills when he wants to find the right person for a management post; he can teach people the right skills, he said. What he looks for in people is good taste and good judgment, a sense for the appropriate, a nose for the fitting, a feel for the right time and the right place.

We can say the same thing about moral choices. We can always teach people the rules. What we hope for to begin with is a person with discernment, the kind of person you can depend on for an appropriate response to the kind of challenges for which there are no rules.

Sometimes it can be a matter of life and death, and of human dignity and human compassion.

Here is an example. Not long ago, a family I know of made a courageous decision to take their baby boy home from the hospital even though the baby was likely to live longer if he had been left in the neonatology unit where all the marvelous tools and talents of medicine were close at hand. They made an appropriate decision—in my judgment—in a situation where rules did not help much.

The situation was this. Their baby had a terrible breathing problem (hyaline membrane disease), and he had to be kept in a respirator to stay alive. But he was born with several other handicaps besides, so that even with a respirator he could not survive for long. How long would he live at the hospital? Nobody knew for sure. Maybe eight months. How long could he live at home? Nobody knew for sure. Maybe a month, or less.

How would he live and die at home? Bathed in love. Touched and talked to. Wept over with tears of infinite care. And cradled in the bosom of family.

How would he die at home? In the presence of those to whom he was tied by the invisible bonds of family love. Given back to God by the mother and father who brought him to life. Before the eyes of a brother and sister who would forever after remember what it was like to love a dying baby brother. And who could ever know for sure what it meant to a newborn baby to die in its mother's arms?

How would he live and die at the hospital? Surrounded by caring professionals. But strangers in white gowns who stayed for a shift and then went home to their own. He would die tied to wires and tubes, hooked to machines. Kept alive a little longer by the best technology available. But dying anyway, only a little later, in a neonatology unit of a huge city hospital.

The family chose to take their baby home, to let their other two children share in loving and caring for a brother who was born to live only long enough to give his family a chance to love him with the passion of someone who knows he can love only for a little while. More, the parents chose to give their baby a chance to live for the precious little while given him in the place where every baby belongs, in the heart of a family.

Before they dismissed the baby to the family's home, the medical staff brooded over the ethics of letting a baby go home where he would most likely die soon, sooner than under the care of the hospital crew. Was it a choice between right and wrong? I don't think so. Do you? It was more like a choice between two right courses, one of which may have been more appropriate than the other. A choice for what best fit the needs of the people whose lives were so deeply touched by it.

I have a hunch that the doctors knew in their own hearts from the outset that the family knew best what was most appropriate for their baby and themselves in their time of sorrow. And they released the baby to the family's care. He died in a circle of abounding love three weeks later.

Appropriateness is usually a matter of more or less, not a

matter of either/or. Sometimes a little more of this and a little less of that can make a difference. But what a difference!

In any case, anyone who wants to make responsible choices does well to ask this question, "Did I do what was appropriate to the unique situation that demanded a hard decision?"

## DOES IT SUPPORT MY COMMITMENTS?

Responsible people dare to make and care to keep commitments. They also know when to break a commitment badly made and wrong to keep.

What do we do when we make a commitment? What sort of a thing is a commitment, and why should we be bound to any we make? We make many kinds of commitments, of course—to people, to causes, to beliefs, to institutions. I will speak of commitments to people.

When we make a commitment to someone, we promise to be with him or her at any unspecified time in the future. We make an open-ended appointment for any tomorrow. We stretch ourselves into the unpredictable future and make one thing predictable: we will be there when needed. No matter what the circumstances are.

When I make a commitment to be with someone, I pledge that I will put my rendezvous with that person ahead of any desire to be somewhere else.

I will change in the time to come. I know she will change too. I will discover later on that I am not the same person I was when I committed myself. I may discover that she is not the same person either. No matter. I intend to keep the commitment regardless of how much I change. Or how much she changes. Our commitment is the only thing about us that will not change.

When we commit ourselves to people, we create an island of certainty for them in the ocean of life's swelling uncertainties. When everything else goes berserk and life seems to be falling apart at the seams, the people we know are given one certainty: We will be there with them. People can count on us when we make commitments and keep them.

Can you imagine what life would be like if nobody could ever give us a promise more firm than "I'll try to make it, but don't count on me"? Nothing works well if we cannot trust people to make firm commitments to do what they promised to do. Or be what they promised to be.

Nobody could run a railroad unless people made and kept commitments. Or a candy factory. Or a country store. Whether you are creating a new nation or planning a family picnic, plotting a corporate merger or arranging a bridal shower, everything depends on whether people are willing to make commitments and keep the commitments they make.

Commitments are the backbone of human relationships, so the question of whether the things we do support or violate our commitments makes or breaks our life together.

When responsible people make a decision, they ask themselves, "How will it impact my significant commitments?" Sometimes the answer is clear, definite, certain. Can selling military secrets to the enemy ever support your commitment to your country? Can having an affair with someone else's spouse ever support your commitment to your own marriage? Can telling your friend's secrets to a third party ever support your commitment to your friendship? Some things seem to subvert some commitments, no matter what the extenuating circumstances are.

But we are not always so sure.

Will you undermine your commitment to your family if you take on an extra job? Will you violate your commitment to your husband if you make friends with an attractive male at the office? Will you be going back on your commitment to your son if he is arrested for selling drugs and you refuse to bail him out? Will you fail your commitment to your country if you refuse to fight in a war that you believe is a wrong war for your country to fight?

Do we not sometimes have to say, "It all depends"?

Whether we can get a clear yes or no answer every time is not the point. In fact, one way to be irresponsible is to act as if the situation is a yes or no situation when it actually is too complicated for either/or answers. When we make believe life is simpler than it really is, we are ducking responsibility.

If we want to act responsibly in iffy situations, where there seems to be no single right answer, one question we need to ask among our repertoire of relevant considerations is, "How will this decision affect my basic commitments?"

No matter how important commitment keeping is, however, we have to be ready to break commitments sometimes.

Some commitments should never be made. And once made ought to be broken as fast as possible. Remember Albert Speer, Hilter's brilliant architect? When he came to the end of the evil road he had traveled and wondered how he could have gone so deeply into Hitler's hell, he came up with this answer: he committed himself to Hitler when he joined the Nazi youth corps and never examined his commitment again.

He could have gotten out early on, but he kept his commitment out of blind, uncritical loyalty to a madman. When Speer finally woke up, too late, and turned against Hitler, the worst accusation Herman Goering, loyal head of Hitler's Luftwaffe, could level at him was "You broke your commitment." Alas, if he had only broken his promise two decades earlier.

A responsible person will keep a steady eye for the difference between surrender and commitment. Whenever someone, especially the leader of a cause, especially a good cause, asks people to surrender their wills to him or her, that leader is asking for a commitment no one should make and no one should keep. When any human being asks for a commitment that is actually a total surrender, it is time to "fold 'em" and walk away.

We do not need to be rigid conservatives to see that life without commitments is chaos. Crazy-making. It is by making commitments that we create community and keep life human in it. Most of the relationships that put warm flesh and blood on the skeletons of our existence require commitments. All of the people who matter most to us are people we have made commitments to. And we break our bond with them and drive them out of their minds, to boot, when they cannot count on us to be there as we promised.

People who keep their bags packed, ready to move out of other people's lives whenever the grass looks greener down the street, leaving those they left behind to pick up the pieces, people who do not care enough to stick it out through long, cold winters with anybody or anything, are usually people who have opted for the self-centered life in which nobody is responsible to anybody.

So one way to test our own responsibility is to ask whether

what we are doing matches up with the important commitments we have made.

## IS IT CONGRUENT WITH MY ROLES?

Sooner or later, we all take on roles. And a responsible person plays out his or her role to the hilt.

We are not talking about playacting, not about pretending, not about make-believe, or wearing masks to hide our real selves. Not that at all. What we are talking about here are real roles in real life.

Some roles are tasks, not masks. Jobs to do, not performances to stage. In the old days we called them callings. What it came to was an inner sense that a person has something to dedicate his or her life to. Our roles are our mission, our métier, our beat.

One person takes on several. For instance, I can be a husband, a father, a professor, a deacon at my church, the president of the local chapter of the NAACP, and, to boot, a troop leader for the Boy Scouts. All of these things that I am and that I do are roles I play in the real life story I am writing with my life.

Each role requires different sorts of things from me. I owe one thing to my wife in my role of husband, another to my church in my role as deacon, another to my students in my role as a teacher, and still another to the NAACP in my role as president of the board.

People can get to know who we really are by the roles we play. People know the real me when they know me as the husband of Doris, the father of Charles, a teacher at Fuller Seminary, a deacon of my church, and a citizen of the United States. Once you have gotten all my roles in your view, you know a lot about me.

I *am* my roles. You *are* your roles.

Not completely. We always keep an inner life at the center that never quite gets captured by our roles. There is an invisible and unique soul tucked inside the roles you play that always stays partly hidden. You are always more than a spouse, more than a bricklayer, more than a chief executive officer. The something more is what makes you a mystery. Such an inexhaustible mystery, and such an interesting one.

Besides, your special inner mystery lets you play your roles in your own unique style.

But even if we are mysteries at bottom, the visible part of us is real too; what people see of us is what they get, and what they see are the roles we play.

Some people think that our roles are disguises, and that the only authentic things about us are our inner lives, our feelings, hankerings, passions. Hang the roles, they will tell you. Your roles are only scaffolding to the real you. Stay in them only as long as they suit you. But when they begin to hem you in and pin you down, when they keep you from being the free-swinging you that you can be if you want to be, drop them the way an actor takes off his or her costume after the final scene. And why not? Why not, if all our roles are only costumes we outgrow if we wear them too long? But are all the roles we play in life only masks that cover our soul's real face?

What do you think?

Could it be that at least a few of our roles in life are the posts we are assigned, tasks we are given so that our lives can fulfill some point and purpose? Could it be that our roles are what put warm flesh and blood on the spare bones of our character? Could it not be that our roles are what we need to give staying power to our loves? And, finally, isn't it true that we need a few steady roles to play so that we can turn our life's script into a durable story with some substance to it?

If we take on some roles as if they were our real selves, we also help make life decent and livable for other people. When we play our roles, other people can trust us to be the same persons for them tomorrow that we are today. What would have happened to us if a few people in our lives had not stuck to their roles?

Roles, freely accepted and faithfully played, are the personal linchpins of any caring community.

So one test of whether we are being responsible is this question: "Am I being congruent with my significant roles?"

There are some things that a responsible man might do if he were single that would not fit his role as a husband if he were married. He could, for instance, spend a long, luscious, and responsible evening dancing with a gorgeous acquaintance from out of town. But if he were married, a long night out even with his secretary might not fit his role as a husband. And if he did it often, he would make life very hard for his wife, make it terribly hard for her to play her own role, mostly because to play her role she needs to trust him to play his.

A rich person can enjoy an afternoon betting at the track, with nobody any the worse off for it. But if a working person with five children risks money on the horses, that would be thumbing his or her nose at that person's most significant role.

It may fit her role when the head of an advertising agency has lunch with her male secretary five times a week; it may undermine his role when a member of the clergy has lunch with his female secretary twice a week. It may fit his role when a staff sergeant orders men to risk their lives for their country; it would conflict with her role if a chief executive officer asked her staff to risk their lives for their company.

True, we tolerate double standards when we say that the roles we play make a difference. Maybe triple or quadruple standards. That is, what's responsible for Jim in his roles in life may be irresponsible for Mary in hers. So what?

It only means that we are dealing with individuals in a beautiful variety of roles, each exploring ways to be responsible to the specific tasks he or she has within the fellowship of the human family. We don't all have to play the same tune; we only need to play our own special tunes as genuine responses to the questions our lives put to us.


## HAVE I USED MY IMAGINATION?

If only evil people did bad things, our world would be a better place to life. The trouble is that good people do a lot of harm, not because they want to hurt somebody, but because they lack imagination. They do not set out to do bad things; they botch the good things they set out to do. And they hurt people because they do not stretch their imagination far enough into the future.

Something happened to me once near Nairobi, Kenya, that taught me how people with good intentions and limited imagination can conspire to give innocent people pain. I had just set out with two friends, a Kenyan and his Canadian wife, and a young woman from the bush on a day's trip from Nairobi up to the village home of my Kenyan friend.

The young woman, maybe seventeen, barefoot, wide-eyed, and very quiet was going with us, back to her village home. She had come down to Nairobi to work in someone's house, but the big city was too much for her to cope with; she was undone by Nairobi's frenzied style, where everyone was a stranger to everyone, and nobody seemed to care; she turned out to be of little good to her citified employers, and they were a disaster for her innocent sense of what human life was all about. So she was coming along with us, back to her loved ones and home, enormously relieved to shake the dust of the city off her feet, and yet afraid that she would be a disappointment to her own family.

We had a six- or seven-hour drive ahead of us, and there would be no fast food shops along the route we were going. So we swallowed hard and decided to trust our luck along the way to find a place to eat. About a half hour out of Nairobi we passed a white frame building with Ionic pillars holding up the tiled roof of its graciously stretched portico. It had the spoiled look of an elegant hotel left over from colonial days. We drove up to it, and asked whether they could serve us lunch. They could and they would be pleased to do it.

We sat down, the four of us looking like an American liberal's dream of a nicely integrated fellowship. We were served with outrageously anachronous colonial dignity. First came a cold drink; the young lady did not touch hers. It took us a few minutes to notice. Then a bowl of soup; she did not lift a hand to a spoon. Now we began to discern what was going on. A sandwich; she hardly gave it a glance. Unpardonably late, we saw that she was terrified.

The village girl, already bruised inside by the ways of big city people, once again was forced to be a misplaced person, alien, infinitely removed from anywhere she belonged, or even felt she could belong. Hurt.

We had made an innocent person suffer. Needlessly. The moral rules we lived by were rules so ingrained in our conscience that we did not pause for an instant to ask whether they were the rules to follow here, at this place, under these special circumstances. The rules were loud and clear: moral people do not leave a village girl in the car while they go into a restaurant to eat their lunch. But rules—the very, very best of rules, rules that all the angels in heaven cordially endorse—rules without imagination can lead moral people to do the devil's work. For they can make the innocent suffer.

With a little imagination, we could have found a better way. We could have asked the maître d' to prepare us some sandwiches that we could have taken with us and eaten together in our car, a group of happy, integrated wanderers.

But we failed. Not because we had the wrong rules, not because we had evil intentions, not because we lacked love, not because we had failed a college course in ethics, but because we did not have enough imagination to feel our way into the mind and heart of a scared girl from a Kenyan village.

In human relationships, imagination is the inward vision of love. It is love's educated guess of what will happen to another person if we do what we think is right. Imagination is compassion stretched beyond our prefabricated notions of right and wrong. Imagination is the beginning of responsible morality.

We fail to use imagination, not because we were not lucky enough to inherit the gift, but because we do not pull ourselves far enough above our own desires, high enough to see ahead into how what we do will touch the lives of people.

Imagination is love's foresight. Without it we are likely to act irresponsibly. So another way to make the responsibility test is to ask, "Did I stop to use imagination before I acted?"


## AM I WILLING TO GO PUBLIC?

We would all stay out of a lot of trouble if we always acted where people could see us. Or if we were at least willing for them to see us. Cover-ups are always the strategy of the irresponsible.

So one way of testing the responsibility of what we are doing is to ask, "Would I be willing to let people I care about know what I am doing?"

A discouraging fact about human nature is that few of us can be trusted for very long to act responsibly behind a curtain. Our yen for cover is a hint that we cannot trust ourselves totally. No wonder darkness and evil are synonymous in almost all religious myths. God is light, said the Apostle John, there is no darkness in him at all. And anyone on earth who loves his neighbor is living in light.

Good things happened after God said, "Let there be light."

How long would illicit love affairs last if lovers met only in well-lit places? How may innocent friendships would become sexual surrenders if the friends never met behind a seal of secrecy?

How many corrupting bribes would be made if they had to be made above the table? How many shady compromises would be offered to politicians if reporters were always listening in?

The test of publicity gives no one absolute security against irresponsibility. Some of us are fools at high noon. And a lot of good things happen at midnight. But when we are being irresponsible, most of us prefer the shadows.

So one way to keep ourselves responsible is to ask, "Would I be willing to make public what I am thinking of doing behind the curtain?"

## AM I WILLING TO ACCEPT THE CONSEQUENCES?

Martin Luther King, Jr., had a strict rule for people who chose to follow his pilgrimage into nonviolent civil disobedience. It was this: anyone who disobeyed unjust laws had to be willing to go to jail for breaking them. You were not to break a law and run for it, evil as the law was; the responsible way was to break the law, stay where you were, and offer yourself to the police.

You had to accept the consequences of civil disobedience even in a righteous cause. If you were not willing to stay at the scene of your "crime," let everybody know what you had done, and take whatever was dished out to you, you were not acting responsibly.

Sticking with the consequences was not a sure test of whether you did the right thing. But it was a fine test of whether you acted responsibly in doing it.

Take a married couple who do not want any more children. Most people would think they did a right thing if they used the pill to avoid conception. But suppose they forgot, or got the dates mixed, and conceived a child. Wouldn't we think that they would be acting most responsibly if they decided to keep, love, and care for a child who was a consequence of their mistake? I try to think of other good examples, but the one I know best is my mother.

She made a choice once to marry her only love, an impractical dreamer of a man, pull her roots out of the soil of her family's ancestral Frisian farm, and hie with him in high hope to the United States of America. Her love died ten tough years later, at the age of thirty-two, leaving her five little ones as her only inheritance, with not a penny to pay the butcher or the baker. And no welfare checks for mothers of dependent children. She was stuck all right, with consequences she did not have in mind when she chose to ship out, third class, with the love of her life, to the land where good dreams were supposed to come true. But she did what people do who accept the consequences of their choices as the raw material for writing the story of their lives: she stuck with what she was stuck with.

So far I have talked about sticking with hard consequences of good choices. Sometimes we redeem bad choices if we stay with the consequences of them. A partner in a trust firm embezzles money to pay his gambling debts. He does a wrong thing. But he admits what he did, commits himself to repay, and shows his good faith by selling his house to make a down payment on redemption. He does not undo the wrongness of his choice; but by accepting consequences he brings some good out of the bad.

Sticking with what we stick ourselves with is the stuff of responsible living. Accepting the consequences of our choices is not a surefire test of whether the choice was good or bad. But it is a quality of character and, long term, the only way to keep life livable after we make our choices.

Living responsibly is a freewheeling challenge. It eludes precise and objective measurement. We are not good judges of one another. I cannot tell you for sure whether you acted responsibly. And you cannot be an infallible judge of whether I acted responsibly. In the last analysis, we have to be our own judges.

And yet there are some tests; I have talked about some of them in this chapter. Acting responsibly is basically a matter of whether we are giving a fitting response to the question that any human situation puts to us. Chances are that we acted responsibly if we

1. Used discernment
2. Interpreted the question before we answered it
3. Considered whether the act was appropriate
4. Used our imagination
5. Checked whether what we did was consistent with our commitments and congruent with our roles in life
6. Were willing to let our acts be seen in public
7. Accepted accountability for the results of what we did

Acting responsibly does not mean that we made *the* only right choice. Tests for acting responsibly are more like checks and balances for the free life than like litmus tests for moral rightness. If we acted responsibly, chances are that we did a good thing under the circumstances. Maybe we even did an excellent thing, maybe only a slightly better thing than anything else we could have done. But it was not necessarily the *only* right thing to do.

Acting responsibly is love's quest for moral excellence in a mixed-up world where life is too complex for infallible formulas, too confusing to give fallible creatures complete certainty that they are always right, and where doing what we are permitted to do is never enough for people who want to do the better thing even more than they want to do the right thing.

# CHAPTER 7

# Being Wrong is Not All Bad

I have made wrong choices and I have made right choices. All things considered, I would really rather make right ones. In fact, I have never met anyone who really liked being in the wrong.

But we have to make choices; that's the rub. There are alternatives. Options. We cannot choose not to choose. Not as long as we are alive in this particular world. For some of us, choices are the hardest part of being real people.

We don't have a choice to make only easy choices. A life of easy choices is a dream, an existence on another planet, not even a human life; in this complex world a lot of our choices come hard.

We all make bad ones. Sometimes. And it's nice to know that bad choices do not have to be fatal.

If you have read this far, you must be convinced that there is no single way, no one and only method of making sure you are doing the right thing.

One way is to follow the rule. Pick the right rule and apply it to your case. We discovered that rules come from many different sources and that only the rules of God and nature are meant for everyone and for always. But there are not enough of these rules to go around. Life's situations are almost infinitely varied and absolute rules are limited.

Another way is to add up the results—the results of actions taken and the likely results of things we think about doing. But this won't always cinch things for us either. We need some standards, some values, to tell us whether the results of our actions are in fact really and truly good, good for the right people, and good at the right time. And to appeal to standards is to appeal beyond the results themselves. We have to ask what our standards are.

Often, maybe mostly, we simply ask whether we are acting responsibly. Are we looking before we leap, thinking before we speak, considering all the angles before we act? If we are, we are probably acting responsibly, which is sometimes almost all we can ask of ourselves. But being responsible does not mean that we are right. It only means that we position ourselves where we have a better crack at doing a reasonably good thing, at least not as bad a thing as we might have done, and maybe the best thing we could do under the circumstances.

In this book, we have been talking about behaving rationally. Making right choices requires keeping our heads on straight, thinking clearly, getting the facts, resorting to rules, calculating consequences, being responsible. It is important to keep our heads clear precisely because life can be so zany.

But a clear head isn't everything.

Don't rule out alternative roads—roads that take us beyond reason—to the right choice.

I know people who have a special knack for making right choices, a special talent for doing right in complex situations, even though they might have had a hard time reading all the way through this book. They have their own special keys to knowledge. Their ways work, too, a lot of the time, not always, but often enough to make life better for people around them most of the time.

Try a few of them.

Some people have intuition.

Call it by another name if you prefer; a hunch, a feeling, a sixth sense, a second sight. Some people simply see with the help of spiritual eyes, hear with the aid of spiritual ears, know with the certainty that comes from a resource lying beneath the mind. And if you are lucky enough to have this power, you should respect it. And use it.

The great Soviet writer Aleksandr Solzhenitsyn was one of thousands upon thousands of innocent people stuck in the Soviet prisons during the terrible Stalin days. He knew that the prison was loaded with spies, that every third prisoner might have been paid to seduce secrets from fellow prisoners and then betray them to the guards. There was no way to know when you were dealing with a spy.

But Solzhenitsyn was never fooled; he spotted them every time, at once, no mistake.

And so he was never taken in.

How did he recognize the spies? He did not know how he did it. He had an intuition. And it worked every time. For him. Other prisoners did not have the gift, and they were suckered by the spies and suffered for it. But Solzhenitsyn respected his own intuition, acted on it, and saved himself considerable misery.

Most of us have moral intuitions. Especially when it comes to recognizing real evil when we see it. Some things people do are so evil that they drum their thumping beat of horror on our souls, and we do not need any intellectual argument to feel it for what it is. Its moral wrongness wallops our inner moral sense; we know it is wrong and nobody has to tell us. We have an intuition.

Don't neglect your own intuitions.

I also recommend prayer, a massively neglected resource for making right choices. It's a simple matter of seeking insight from God. Not a lazy mind's resort to magic, not at all. Just a way of tapping into a wisdom better than ours.

There was one person in my life whom I would trust to make right choices in some moral dilemmas that boggle the minds of experts. Not in every complicated case, mind you, not in matters that needed a sophisticated grasp of technical details. But in situations where ordinary people got confused, she always seemed to plow right through to the heart of the matter, to the gut issues, the human issues that counted most for real people, and she somehow knew what was right.

I am talking about my mother again. A woman thoroughly innocent of learning, she never went to school beyond the fourth or fifth grade. My mother was not a notably rational individual: she went by feeling; feeling was her being. And she did not have a lot of confidence even in her feelings.

Maybe because she did not know what else to do, she prayed a lot.

There was a bedroom in our house tucked just off the

kitchen. Anyone lying awake in bed there could hear everything people were saying in the kitchen. And at our house all the business that needed to be talked about was done in the kitchen. I often slept in that bedroom; I could hear everything. The last thing I heard every night was the urgent SOS that my mother registered with heaven as her last act before she went to sleep.

She would get on her knees in front of a rickety kitchen chair, grab hold of the edges, holding on for life itself, the way a drowning person grabs hold of a floating board among the flotsam of the sea, and she would pour it all out—in her native language, Frisian, understood only in heaven and in Friesland—to the God she believed had a special spot in his large heart for poor, hard-working widows with five little children to feed and who would, if it was his will, steer her in the right way. I don't think she could have made it without those nightly prayers, which, come to think of it, were more like moanings from the soul's subterranean cells than like words formed by a rational mind.

Prayer sensitized her inner mind, gave her recourse to a wisdom that was generated below or behind the resources of the intellect, set her in tune with the God whose will is the heart and soul of all right choices.

It made her wise where others smarter than she were fools.

She had a nose for what was mean, she recognized the cheap shot before it took off, and she always had the sense to avoid it. But what was more remarkable was her talent for recognizing the more excellent way. We sometimes thought people took advantage of her. But they didn't, not really, they just got the benefits of my mother's taste for excellence.

There was old Mrs. Ratsouer, for instance, a lonely, neurotic woman, who never combed her hair and whose stockings curled beneath her knees—a bit daft, if the neighborhood grapevine had it right. She lived alone, in a ramshackle house down the street from ours. She was scared stiff to live there. And she did not have anybody to take her in. What kin she had would not have much to do with her.

My mother took Mrs. Ratsouer in, gave her a room to sleep in, ate with her and talked with her at night, and mostly just let her be near somebody with a patient heart and gentle touch. We were sure my mother was being taken in by a crafty old neurotic who was manipulating a kind lady who was too generous to say no to her. We tried to convince my mother to leave the poor woman to her own relatives. We tried to convince her that she was making a bad choice.

But my mother was not being taken in. She knew what was going on. Nobody was kidding her. She was making a choice for human excellence when the rest of us were content with the mediocrity of self-interest.

I think she learned to recognize the more excellent way during those praying sessions in the kitchen at night when the lights were out and the kids were all in bed.

She never developed a taste for what people with less feel for excellence call the good life. But when she was buried, you would have thought a notable public figure had passed on. So many people came to her funeral; the number took us all by surprise. They packed the chapel, white people, black people, people from the neighborhood and people from way across town, people we had never seen before along with old friends of the family, people who had crossed her path and been touched by her unschooled sense for excellence, and did not forget. They came there because they wanted to remember a woman who learned at prayer how to make excellent choices.

Don't discount the power of prayer for making right choices.

Some people put stock in their traditions. They are lucky for having traditions to put stock in, and wise for respecting them.

Remember the fiddler on the roof? A little man in a long green coat, standing on a steep roof, on one foot, playing his fiddle without falling off the slippery shingles. He stands for all of us, trying to play the right notes in life without falling down and breaking our necks—trying to make a little music out of our lives, trying to do the right thing.

And how do we keep our balance? "I'll tell you," sang Tevye in *Fiddler on the Roof*, "in one word, I'll tell you, *tradition!* Because of our tradition, everybody knows who he is and what God expects him to do."

We don't have to pretend that all traditions are sacred, and we don't have to be slaves to our traditions. Traditions don't tell us everything. And they can lead us wrong now and then. But they are still a pretty good bet. If someone asks you why you made a certain decision, and you tell them, "This is the way my people have always done it," you are not necessarily talking nonsense.

Tradition is a treasury of human experience; it can be a signal from God. Only fools and prophets can afford to ignore tradition. Most of us fall somewhere in between.

Finally, it is not a bad idea to listen to moral authorities.

There have been and still are inspired people; in moral matters, we need their help. Men and women have been inspired to speak the truth about how we should live. This is why we still look to the Bible for direction.

But people are inspired, too, in living ways, not the ways of words, but the ways of life; their life is their message. There are special people who have embroidered the tapestry of human history by their inspired lives. I think of people like St. Francis, Martin Luther King, Jr., Dietrich Bonhoeffer, Mother Teresa, and thousands of inspired people whose messages never get beyond their own neighborhoods. Maybe your uncle or your grandfather, or you. These are people worth listening to if only because in their brief time in a shadowy world they burn a candle of moral excellence to light up life a little for the rest of us. They leave us memories of noble choices when excellence was bought with a price of pain. And they help us ordinary people to make excellent choices in our ordinary places.

Don't ignore the inspired people, their writings, their lives.

We are not on our own. We have resources.

But, even then, after we have thought, after we have prayed, after we have explored inspired wisdom and consulted our tradition, we do not always know for sure. We can make bad mistakes.

Not knowing for sure is not the worst thing that can happen to us. And being wrong is not all that bad.

For one thing, doubt is simply an experience of our limits, the limits of our wisdom amid the complexity of life. Our doubts are nothing more than humility in the face of reality. And humility is a signal of an angel telling us to look before we leap. The humility of simple doubt can save a doubter from disaster.

The cocksure of the world are the ones I worry about. The person who never hesitates to tell you what's right, who always knows, who never needs to look at both sides of the question, who never shudders in the shadow of doubt, this is the person to watch out for. People like this have lost touch with their own fallible humanity. And they have set themselves up for a fall.

We can make mistakes. We can miss the right turn. We make wrong choices. Count on it, you are not always going to do the right thing. As if you didn't know.

So it's important to know that making wrong choices is not the worst thing that can happen to you.

I must tell you now, as we come to the end of our journey together, what I think is the most important part of making choices, the bottom line, what matters most.

It is the possibility of being forgiven.

Morality is the need to make right choices. Forgiveness is the freedom to make wrong choices.

Dare to be wrong! Risk it! With forgiveness you discover that being wrong is not all that bad. No wrong choice you make can persuade God to love you less. Believe this and you will have new courage to make choices even when you are not sure they will be the right ones to make. Courage to fail.

Søren Kierkegaard, that complicated Danish philosopher, once said a prayer that went something like this:

Lord, I have to make a choice, and I'm afraid that I may make the wrong one. But I have to make it anyway; and I can't put it off. So I will make it, and trust you to forgive me if I do wrong. And, Lord, I will trust you, too, to help make things right afterward. Amen.

The last word about choices is this: nothing you do wrong can get God to love you less than he did when you did things right. Nothing need ever separate you from the love of God. After all is said and done, being right is not the most important thing in the world. Being forgiven is.